Vegetation Community Monitoring Protocol for the Heartland Inventory and Monitoring Network

Natural Resource Report NPS/HTLN/NRR—2009/141

Kevin M. James, Mike D. DeBacker, Gareth A. Rowell, Jennifer L. Haack and Lloyd W. Morrison

National Park Service
Heartland I&M Network
Wilson's Creek National Battlefield
6424 West Farm Road 182
Republic, MO 65738

August 2009

U.S. Department of the Interior
National Park Service
Natural Resource Program Center
Fort Collins, Colorado

The National Park Service, Natural Resource Program Center publishes a range of reports that address natural resource topics of interest and applicability to a broad audience in the National Park Service and others in natural resource management, including scientists, conservation and environmental constituencies and the public.

The Natural Resource Report Series is used to disseminate high-priority, current natural resource management information with managerial application. The series targets a general, diverse audience and may contain NPS policy considerations or address sensitive issues of management applicability.

All manuscripts in the series receive the appropriate level of peer review to ensure that the information is scientifically credible, technically accurate, appropriately written for the intended audience and designed and published in a professional manner.

Views, statements, findings, conclusions, recommendations and data in this report are those of the author(s) and do not necessarily reflect views and policies of the National Park Service, U.S. Department of the Interior. Mention of trade names or commercial products does not constitute endorsement or recommendation for use by the National Park Service.

This report is available from the Heartland I&M Network website (http://www.nature.nps.gov/im/units/HTLN) and the Natural Resource Publications Management website (http://www.nature.nps.gov/publications/NRPM).

Please cite this publication as:

James, K. M., M. D. DeBacker, G. A. Rowell, J. L. Haack and L. W. Morrison. 2009. Vegetation community monitoring protocol for the Heartland Inventory and Monitoring Network. Natural Resource Report NPS/HTLN/NRR—2009/141. National Park Service, Fort Collins, Colorado.

NPS 920/100249, August 2009

Contents

Figures

Tables

Appendices

Acknowledgements

The National Park Service's Inventory and Monitoring Program provided funding for vegetation community monitoring protocol development and continues to fund monitoring across Heartland Inventory and Monitoring Network parks. The original edition of the protocol "Vegetation Community Monitoring Protocol for the Heartland I&M Network and Prairie Cluster Prototype Monitoring Program" was written in 2004 by Michael DeBacker, Alicia Sasseen, Dr. Gareth Rowell, Cindy Becker, Lisa P. Thomas, John Boetsch and Dr. Gary D. Willson. Peer review of the original protocol was conducted by Northern Prairie Science Center and benefited from the comments of Diane Larson, Jim Stubbendieck, Wes Newton, Jan Keough, Melinda Smith, Gerry Steinauer, Kristin Legg, David Glen-Lewin and Don Faber-Langendoen. We have updated the protocol to reflect the network's coordinated monitoring efforts among terrestrial projects and the turning over of Agate Fossil Beds National Monument and Scotts Bluff National Monument to the Northern Great Plains Inventory and Monitoring Network. This protocol uses sections of text without citation from the original protocol. Numerous NPS staff and volunteers have contributed to the development of this protocol. Therefore, the list of authors simply reflects those who put down on paper the work of this larger group.

Background and Objectives

Issues Being Addressed and Rationale for Monitoring Vegetation Communities

Native and restored plant communities are part of the foundation of park ecosystems and provide a natural backdrop to cultural events in parks throughout the Heartland Inventory and Monitoring Network (HTLN). Even for cultural parks that contain natural communities, conserving those communities is important as land conversion and habitat fragmentation increases across the landscape around parks in the Heartland Network. As large tracks of natural vegetation communities are lost, the communities within parks become representative of once widespread or locally unique community types that warrant special attention through long-term monitoring and coordinated management.

Long-term ecological monitoring, while contributing to our empirical understanding of plant communities, is integral to the proper management and protection of the lands entrusted to the National Park Service (NPS). Resource managers of the parks require an effective plant community monitoring protocol to assess their management strategies in maintaining and/or restoring prairies, savanna-woodland and forest community composition and structure. Our monitoring strategy attempts to balance the immediate needs of managers for current information and the need for insight into the changes occurring in vegetation communities over time. Vegetation communities across the Heartland Network are primarily of three types: tallgrass prairie, deciduous savanna-woodland and deciduous forest. Each of these three types of communities has been impacted over much of the prior two centuries. Land conversion, habitat fragmentation, invasion of non-native species and disruption or elimination of the natural disturbance regime has resulted in limiting or altering their extent and quality. Scientists estimate the loss of native prairie ranges from 80 to 99.9%, with the greatest losses occurring in the tallgrass prairie and oak savanna communities. Further, only 71% of shortgrass prairie and 59% of mixed-grass prairie remain (Knopf and Samson 1997).

Grassland ecosystems are maintained by a complex disturbance regime including frequent large- and small-scale disturbances. The interactive effect of periodic fire and ungulate grazing is widely recognized as a critical component of the natural disturbance regime in tallgrass prairie ecosystems (Bragg 1995, Davison and Kindscher 1999, Howe 1999, Collins 2000). These in turn interact with interannual climate variation to affect spatial and temporal dynamics (Collins 1987, Knapp and Seastedt 1998, Knapp *et al.* 1999, Collins 2000). Due to the complex disturbance regimes, grassland systems consist of dynamic mosaics of vegetation patches scattered across the landscape, highly variable in both space and time (Collins and Glenn 1991, Collins and Glenn 1997, Collins 2000, Fuhlendorf and Engle 2001).

Similar to grassland ecosystems, oak-hickory forests developed under a complex disturbance regime. Oak savannas form transition zones within the eastern prairie while oak-hickory forests once formed large tracts across the landscape from southern Arkansas to northern Iowa and east to Ohio (McShea and Healy 2002). Oak-hickory communities can be thought of as being in a constant state of recovery from varying degrees of natural disturbances (Johnson et al 2002). However, with the elimination or control of fire, much of the natural disturbance regime has been changed, which is currently reflected in the composition and structure of these forests (Nelson 2005). Understanding both the dominant cover types of the forests and their structural characteristics provides insight into the recent disturbance history of the forest stand and yields information that can be used for silvicutural management (Oliver and Larson 1996). Further monitoring of tree seedling and sapling regeneration can act as a predictor of future forest cover types (Eyre 1980). Monitoring the structural stages along with the natural and managed disturbance regimes can be used to develop management strategies that consider multiple successional trajectories at the forest stand scale.

Prairie communities exhibit high year-to-year fluctuations in species composition and abundance; however, in stable systems, the community structure remains constant over long time frames or large spatial scales (Collins 2000, Earnest and Brown 2001). Savanna-woodland systems exhibit less annual variability yet fluctuate between prairie dominated understory and increasing canopy cover as affected by natural disturbance and succession. Forested systems show change in species composition at a slower time scale in the absence of disturbance, yet can exhibit more immediate changes following large gap-forming disturbances. Long-term studies of plant communities and individual species are needed to determine appropriate temporal and spatial scales at which plant communities can be considered stable (Collins 2000).

When considering the larger landscape and ecosystems of the region it becomes important to monitor natural and restored vegetation communities on National Park Service lands within the HTLN. Understanding long-term trends of native plant species richness and abundance is critical as ecosystems become increasingly altered or disappear. Information gathered over time will improve the understanding of vegetation community patterns and processes as well as assess the effects of management actions.

Historical Development of Vegetation Monitoring in Network Parks
Initiated in 1994, the Prairie Cluster Prototype Long-Term Ecological Monitoring Program (PC-LTEM) was established to address monitoring concerns in National Park Service prairie parks in the Great Plains. From 1994 – 1999 the PC-LTEM, in collaboration with the USGS-Biological Resources Division, initiated pilot studies in six geographically distinct prairie parks to develop a long-term vegetation monitoring protocol. In addition to providing needed information on the status of national prairie resources, a monitoring protocol for six prairie parks was designed to address long-term changes in vegetation occurring under different management strategies (Wilson et al 2002).

The PC-LTEM park units are Agate Fossil Beds National Monument (AGFO), Effigy Mounds National Monument (EFMO), Homestead National Monument of America (HOME), Pipestone National Monument (PIPE), Scotts Bluff National Monument (SCBL), Tallgrass Prairie National Preserve (TAPR) (added in 1997) and Wilson's Creek National Battlefield (WICR). Located along an east-west precipitation gradient and a north-south temperature gradient, these parks capture much of the climatic and biotic variability of all parks in the Great Plains, containing short-grass prairie (AGFO and SCBL), tallgrass prairie (TAPR, HOME, EFMO and PIPE) and savanna-woodland sites (EFMO and WICR). PC-LTEM serves as a testing ground for long-term monitoring, emphasizing the development of sound monitoring protocols, attention to data management and data quality issues and regular reporting of results to management.

In 2001, the NPS implemented park vital signs monitoring programs in approximately 270 natural resource parks. The NPS organized these parks into 32 networks, linked by geography and shared natural resource characteristics. The Heartland Network was created to service fifteen parks in eight Midwestern states representing tallgrass prairie, Ozark highlands and eastern deciduous forest ecoregions. Initially co-located with the PC-LTEM program, the two programs were further integrated in 2003. Collectively the two programs form The Heartland Inventory and Monitoring Network (HTLN).

The HTLN park units are: Arkansas Post National Memorial (ARPO), Buffalo National River (BUFF), Cuyahoga Valley National Park (CUVA), Effigy Mounds National Monument (EFMO), George Washington Carver National Monument (GWCA), Herbert Hoover National Historic Site (HEHO), Homestead National Monument of America (HOME), Hopewell Culture National Historic Park (HOCU), Hot Springs National Park (HOSP), Lincoln Boyhood National Monument (LIBO), Ozark National Scenic Riverways (OZAR), Pea Ridge National Military Park (PERI), Pipestone National Monument (PIPE), Tallgrass Prairie National Preserve (TAPR) and Wilson's Creek National Battlefield (WICR) (Figure 1). Five of the PC-LTEM Program parks (EFMO, HOME, PIPE, TAPR, WICR) are included within the HTLN.

The culmination of the PC-LTEM and vital signs monitoring program collaboration was a vegetation monitoring protocol for the Heartland Inventory and Monitoring Network (DeBacker et al 2004). With the merger of the two programs, vegetation monitoring of forested communities was expanded to include HOSP and PERI in 2007. Vegetation monitoring occurs at nine HTLN parks: EFMO, GWCA, HEHO, HOME, HOSP, LIBO, PERI, PIPE, TAPR and WICR.

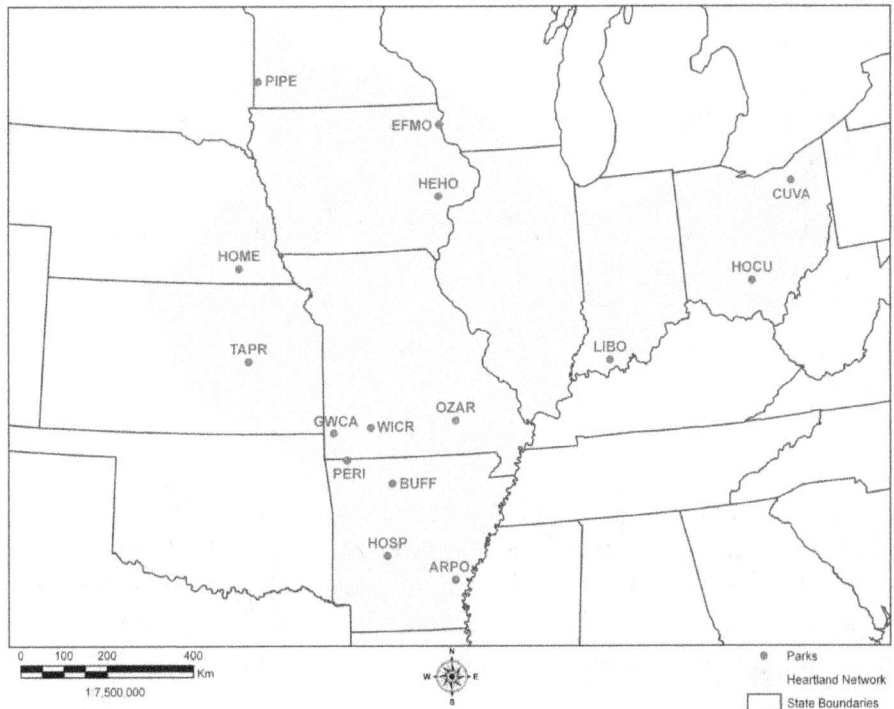

Figure 1. The Heartland Inventory and Monitoring Network park units.

Two of the original seven PC-LTEM parks, AGFO and SCBL will be transferred to the Northern Great Plains Network (NGPN) in 2009. Vegetation monitoring by the HTLN will cease after the 2009 field season and data will be transferred to the NGPN along with monitoring responsibility.

Initially vegetation sampling occurred during two consecutive years at a park and was followed by a three-year interval of no sampling. To facilitate monitoring integration among other HTLN terrestrial projects the revisit design was changed to match the breeding bird sampling schedule (Peitz et al 2008). Beginning in 2009, parks are sampled during a single year with a three-year interval between sampling events (i.e., once every four years). Furthermore, breeding bird monitoring, invasive exotic plant species monitoring and vegetation community monitoring now occur at the same parks during the same year.

In addition to the revisit design, the logistics of sampling prairie parks has changed. Prior to the 2009 field season, prairie parks were sampled twice during the field season to collect data throughout the growing season. To facilitate efficient data collection, data management, analysis and reporting prairie parks are now sampled once during the early summer growing season (during the same time as the original sampling prior to 2009). Further discussion and justification for these changes can be found in Appendices A and B, respectively.

Measurable Objectives

Vegetation community monitoring in the HTLN parks is designed to detect and describe changes in prairie, savanna-woodland and forested communities. There are three primary objectives for the monitoring defined in this protocol:

1. Describe the species composition, structure and diversity of prairie, savanna-woodland and forested communities;

2. Determine temporal changes in the species composition, structure and diversity of prairie, savanna-woodland and forested communities;

3. Determine the relationship between temporal and spatial changes and environmental variables including specific management practices.

Sampling Design

Response Design

The HTLN vegetation community monitoring protocol is based on the National Science Foundation's Konza Prairie Long-Term Ecological Research Program. For the HTLN, the primary sample unit consists of two permanent, parallel 50 m transects with five sets of nested plots systematically spaced along each transect (Figure 2). The transect pair is the primary sample unit and is referred to throughout the protocol as the site. The plot is the secondary sample unit.

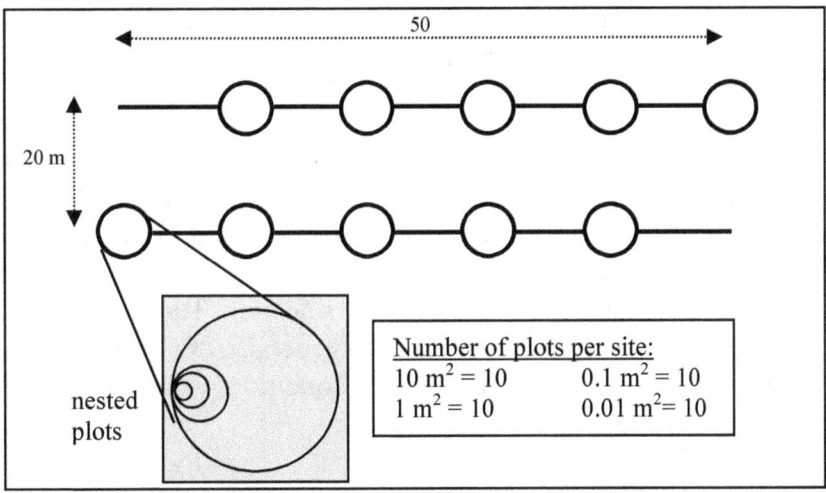

Figure 2. The Heartland Inventory and Monitoring Network vegetation community monitoring site comprised of two, 50 m long transects with ten sets of nested plots systematically arranged.

The plots are used to collect ground flora data. Working from the smallest to the largest plot, all herbaceous, woody shrub and tree seedling and sapling species are identified. Foliar cover is estimated in the 10 m² plot using a modified Daubenmire scale. Trees less than 5.0 cm diameter at breast height (dbh) are tallied by species. For analysis, the site is used as the unit of replication and individual plots within the site are pooled or averaged. The 0.1 ha area between the two transects is used to collect data on the woody species greater than 5.0 cm dbh in the understory and overstory canopy layers. Diameter at breast height is measured for each individual tree greater than 5.0cm.

From the site data, summary variables are calculated. Summary variables include: (1) plant species richness and diversity, (2) the ratio of exotic to native species, (3) species abundance and frequency, (4) woody species density and basal area, (5) overstory canopy cover and (6) ground cover characteristics. Changes in these summary variables are used to detect trends over time in the vegetation community.

Data collection methods are discussed in brief in Section III. Field Methods are discussed in detail in SOP #5 "Measuring Frequency and Cover of Herbaceous and Shrub Species", SOP #7 "Measuring Ground Cover and SOP #8 "Conducting the Woody Species Sampling". Analyses of data for both annual status and temporal trends are discussed in Section IV and SOP #12 "Data Summary and Analysis."

Spatial Design

Overview of Spatial Design
To effectively use limited monitoring resources, information derived from a relatively small number of sites must be used to infer changes over a much larger area. For the inference to be valid, a probability based sample design within a defined reference frame is required. This section describes a stratified, random spatial design that serves as general guidance for locating

monitoring sites. From time to time, deviations from this general approach are required to accommodate specific circumstances on the ground.

Defining the Reference Frame

The many different vegetation types, management practices and park specific data needs, as well as the logistical constraints related to field work, prohibit comprehensive sampling at each park. This prevents simply treating the park as the area of interest. In choosing smaller subsets of the park as the reference frame, park-specific resource management issues and/or the desire to capture landscape and community heterogeneity guide the selection. The smaller subset is the reference frame for which statistical inference is made. In general, areas that represent a range of community types (prairie, savanna-woodland and forest), conditions (high-quality remnants, restoration areas) and/or management strategies are selected.

Table 1. National park units, reference frames and the community types sampled within a reference frame.

Park	Reference frame	Community type
EFMO	Prairie restoration	Tallgrass prairie
	Goat prairies	Savanna
	Forest: north and south units	Eastern deciduous forest
GWCA	Prairie restoration	Tallgrass prairie
HEHO	Prairie restoration	Tallgrass prairie
HOME	Prairie restoration	Tallgrass prairie
	Forest	Lowland riparian forest
HOSP	Sugarloaf Mountain area	Oak-hickory-pine forest
PERI	Natural area	Oak-hickory forest
PIPE	Sioux quartzite prairie	Sioux quartzite prairie
	Prairie restoration	Tallgrass prairie
	Native prairie	Tallgrass prairie
TAPR	Grazing pastures	Tallgrass prairie
WICR	Manley Woodland	Oak–hickory woodland
	Prairie restoration	Tallgrass prairie

Stratifying within the Reference Frame

The need for vegetation monitoring at parks throughout the HTLN necessitates a sample design that effectively and efficiently provides detailed species- and community-level data that can address changes in the community over time. The sample methods employed involve species-level measures, necessitating small sample sizes. Stratification by physical features such as landscape position, soils and geology provide an effective *a priori* approach to an efficient, equal distribution of sites within a reference frame.

In small, homogenous study units with little topographic variability, soils alone are used to stratify the reference frame. In larger areas characterized by greater topographic gradients, aspect is used along with soil to stratify the reference frame. In a GIS, aspect is determined by using a digital elevation model to classify areas in the reference frame as dry and southerly (>135 and <315 degrees) or northerly (<135 and >315). These cutoff points are based on the Beers transformation that accounts for southwest facing slopes often being the driest (Beers *et al.* 1966). See Appendix C for park reference frames and monitoring site locations.

Deploying Monitoring Sites

The number of sites to be deployed within a reference frame is made on a case-by-case basis. Factors include field work logistics, expense and professional judgment regarding the adequacy of a particular sample size in representing the community within the reference frame. Once the total sample size is determined, monitoring sites are distributed among strata proportionate to each stratum's area within the reference frame.

A general approach for deploying sites begins with establishing a grid overlay of the reference frame. The vertices of the grid are spatially referenced to form a matrix of potential monitoring points. Soil and aspect attributes are assigned to each vertex using a GIS to identify a pool of potential sites for each. In the field, points are visited in random order. When arriving at a point, the suitability of the area as a monitoring site is assessed (a point may be considered unsuitable if it is influenced by an unnatural occurrence such as a trail.) If the point is suitable, a permanent monitoring location is established. Alternatively, the reason for rejection is noted and the next point is visited until all monitoring sites are established. Details relating to establishing monitoring sites are described in SOP #4, "Establishing and Marking Permanent Sample Sites." Sites are physically marked on the ground and located in the field with a GPS unit (see SOP #3 "Using GPS" and SOP #4 "Establishing and Marking Sampling Plots" for instruction regarding GPS navigation and site establishment.)

Sampling Frequency and Replication

In developing a logistical plan, the timing of sampling within the growing season is considered, with sampling limited to late May through July. Plant communities are sampled at approximately the same time each year to help differentiate long-term trends in foliar cover from changes attributable to within-season variability.

Sampling is spread throughout a growing season in the following manner: spring/early summer sampling in prairie communities with mid-summer sampling in woodland-savanna and forested communities.

All sites within a reference frame are sampled for a single year followed by a three-year interval without sampling (Table 2). This design is well suited for trampling-sensitive systems such as prairies and savannas, allows for a greater number of sites to be visited through time and coordinates sampling schedules among other terrestrial monitoring projects. Additional sampling occurs at TAPR to monitor the effects of a specific and targeted management regime in a portion of the park.

At EFMO, forested sites are sampled based on fire management unit and timing of prescribed fire. Sampling occurs immediately following a prescribed fire and once again prior to the next scheduled fire for the fire management unit. Following a complete sampling rotation of all forested sites (2009), the annual rotating panel design will be re-evaluated.

In this protocol, the reference frame within parks remains the framework for statistical interest. Analysis and results are not extrapolated to multiple parks or comparison of similar communities among parks. Additionally, every 15 to 20 years, sites will be assessed for trampling effect and subject to subsequent replacement if necessary (T. McDonald, personal communication).

Table 2. Sampling schedule for vegetation community monitoring in the Heartland Inventory and Monitoring Network parks, 2008 through 2016. All parks are visited on a [1-3] sampling schedule with the exception of EFMO and TAPR.

Region (Parks)	2008	2009	2010	2011	2012	2013	2014	2015	2016
Ozarks-prairie (WICR–GWCA)	X				X				X
Prairie-savanna (HOME–PIPE– EFMO–HEHO)		X				X			
Tallgrass prairie (TAPR)			X	X			X	X	
Ozarks-forest (WICR–PERI–HOSP)					X				X
Eastern forest (EFMO)	X	X	X	X	X	X	X	X	X

Rationale for Selected Design

Monitoring objectives are integral to defining the sampling design. The sample design for vegetation community monitoring is driven by two main goals: 1) to assess the status of vegetation communities by estimating community parameters at distinct points in time and 2) detecting trends in vegetation communities over time by measuring net change in certain parameters.

1. *The selected design is appropriate for long-term monitoring in grassland systems.* This is a modified version of the sampling design employed by the National Science Foundation Long-Term Ecological Research (LTER) program at Konza Prairie, a long-term ecological research program in tallgrass prairie. Ongoing and prior research at Konza Prairie LTER (Gibson 1988, Collins and Glenn 1991, Glenn and Collins 1992, Collins 1992) demonstrates that permanently located 10 m^2 plots (i.e., our secondary sample unit) are effective for investigating community-level change in prairie communities. Repeated measures of the same location allow for differentiation of site and year factors, essential to measuring trend through time (Lesica and Steele 1996, Elzinga *et al.* 1998).

2. *The selected design is appropriate for savanna-woodland and forested systems.* A prioritized interest in addressing management and restoration efforts in savanna and forested systems led to a sampling design that provides information on woody regeneration and the overstory strata. The rectangular 0.1 ha area within the paired transects serves as an overstory plot and data on regeneration is collected in the 10 m^2 plots. The overstory sampling is consistent with techniques used in the fire effects program in forested areas (USDI National Park Service 2003).

3. *The selected design accommodates habitats of varying size.* The sample design is adjustable to accommodate large and small study units. The number of sites established is dependent on habitat and community diversity within the study unit. In small study units, sampling consistency is retained by reducing the site to a single transect, or reducing the length of the paired transects. Conversely, in large study units, sample units are spatially distributed using habitat stratification and randomization.

4. *The selected design addresses species-level dynamics.* Within each 10 m^2 plot, the three nested plots (0.01 m^2, 0.1 m^2 and 1.0 m^2) are comparable to a nested frequency frame used by The Nature Conservancy and the square plot design suggested by Peet *et al.* (1998) for plant community monitoring. Nested plots are capable of detecting shifts in frequency by optimizing the spatial scale (Elzinga *et al.* 1998).

5. *The selected design is easy to learn and use.* Field procedures are easy to use and repeatable over time by different sampling crews. Implementation does not require extensive time or costly equipment. Furthermore, transects increase the efficiency of finding and sampling a number of permanent plots quickly (Thompson 1992). The association of plots with permanent transect lines facilitates accurate relocation and measurement.

6. *The spatial design offers the flexibility of a stratified random approach; however, has the grid infrastructure as an underlying feature.* The underlying grid offers two advantages. First, it ensures that any two sites will not be closer to one another than the grid cell size. Second, the grid provides an infrastructure for other studies that may be more suited to systematic sampling, thus providing some potential for co-location between vegetation monitoring sites and those of other studies (See chapter 4 in DeBacker *et al.* 2005).

7. *The sequence of sampling tours allows for the greatest amount of field work to be accomplished per year while minimizing cost.* The one-year-on, three-year-off revisit plan protects sites from trampling effects while providing three consecutive years for resource managers to implement management actions.

8. *The selected design-based approach to monitoring is advantageous over model-based approaches.* Design-based approaches are objective, unbiased and free of assumptions, whereas model-based analyses require a model and assumptions to make estimates and extrapolate results to non-sampled areas. Design-based analyses use a rigorous probability sample instead of assumptions to make estimates and extrapolate to non-sampled areas. The objectivity and unbiased nature of design-based approaches are especially important in studies where the results are often contentious.

Field Methods

Field Season Preparations, Field Schedule and Equipment Setup

Prior to the field season each year the crew members should review this entire protocol, including all of the SOPs. Crew leaders should pay special attention to equipment listed in SOP #1 "Preparations and Equipment Setup Prior to the Field Season." All of the equipment and supplies listed in SOP #1 should be organized and made ready for the field season.

Review of plant identification using both live and dead plant material is particularly important each year. Plant misidentifications are difficult to trace once the summer field season begins and the learning curve in the field is greatly buffered with pre-field study. SOP #2 "Training Observers" contains information for the crew leader and crew members to gauge the level of quality expected.

The revisit plan outlined in Section II, "Overall Survey Design" of this protocol defines the park sequence to be scheduled each year. Sampling dates should be scheduled and logistics organized prior to the start of each field season. Staff workloads and unpredictable weather necessitate maintaining some flexibility in scheduling the sequence and duration of sampling trips.

Sampling Methods

The crew leader decides the sequence of sites to be sampled in the field. Once arriving at the park, park maps, a GPS unit and a metal detector are used to locate each site. The ends of both 50 meter long transects are permanently monumented with reinforced metal bars (rebar) during site establishment and aid in relocation of the site. The rebar, sunk into the ground with the upper 4 – 6 inches exposed, are tagged with a metal tag imprinted with the site number, transect letter (A or B) and transect start (S) or finish (F) designation.

Each day the crew leader splits the team into pairs, matching an observer with a scribe. The scribe is responsible for ensuring all data listed on the data sheets are collected, including plot metadata. The observer is responsible for species identification and cover estimates. Pairing observers allows equal opportunity for all team members to work on all components of sampling, reduces observer exhaustion and breaks up monotony. Furthermore, changing the make-up of sampling pairs reduces divergent estimates of foliar cover and increases consistent recording and tracking of unknown specimens.

All sampling begins at the start of each transect to avoid errors in labeling plots on the data sheet. Along transect A, plots are centered at 10 m, 20 m, 30 m, 40 m and 50 m. Along transect B, plots are centered at 0 m, 10 m, 20 m, 30 m and 40 m. Refer to SOP #4 "Establishing and Marking Permanent Sample Sites" for instructions pertaining to accurate transect and plot placement.

Each team is responsible for keeping track of the equipment and data sheets. Before leaving any site, all equipment is accounted for and data sheets are checked and passed on to the crew leader. When leaving the field each day, data sheets are again checked for completeness and readability. The project manager is responsible for the safekeeping and organization of the data sheets and ensuring data entry. A trip report including weather conditions, logistical problems, any subsequent departure from the protocol, species identification problems, etc. should be written by the project manager upon conclusion of each monitoring trip.

Collecting the Circular Plot Data

For each 10 m^2 circular plot, the ground-level cover of bare soil, bare rock, tree leaf litter, grass litter and woody debris is estimated using the modified Daubenmire cover value scale (Daubenmire 1959, Table 3). Each individual percentage value alone cannot exceed 100%, but when combined the cover value for a plot may be greater than 100% due to layering at the ground-level. These attributes are measured in circular plots to describe changes in ground cover and allow for exploration of the correlative relationships between compositional changes and environmental attributes.

After collecting ground-level cover estimates, the observer nests the 0.01 m², 0.1 m² and 1.0 m² circular plots within the 10 m² plots. Beginning with the 0.01 m² plot, all species rooted in the plot are identified. Once all species in the plot are recorded, the observer moves onto the 0.1 m² plot. Only species not observed in the .01 m² plot are recorded. This is repeated in the 1.0 m² plot and then in the 10 m² plot. Once species presence has been recorded, the observer estimates foliar cover for each species in the entire 10 m² plot. Only species rooted in the plot are included in estimates of foliar cover. A reference list provided for each plot lists the names, but not the associated cover values, of species previously collected in the plot. Comparison with the cumulative plot species list maintains consistency in species identification and creates a check for missing species.

Foliar cover serves as the estimate of abundance for herbaceous and multi-stemmed shrub species. Foliar cover is defined as the area occupied by the perpendicular projection of the aerial parts of individuals of the plant species under consideration to the ground (Greig-Smith 1983). A cover class index modified from Daubenmire (1959, Table 3 is used for all cover estimates. Using cover classes reduces the problem of observer-bias through partitioning all possible values into seven classes with broader cover classes in the middle of the scale and narrower cover classes at the lower and upper ends of the scale. Details of how to conduct cover estimates and for filling in data forms are given in SOP #5 "Measuring Frequency and Cover of Herbaceous and Shrub Species" and SOP #7 "Measuring Ground Cover."

Table 3. Modified Daubenmire cover value scale.

Cover Class Codes	Range of Cover (%)
7	95-100
6	75-95
5	50-75
4	25-50
3	5-25
2	1-5
1	0-0.99

Collecting Woody Vegetation Data

In woodland communities (EFMO, HOME, HOSP, PERI and WICR), stem density is used to estimate abundance of tree species. Seedling and sapling information is collected in each 10 m² plot and tree data (individual trees ≥ 5.0cm dbh) are collected within a rectangular 0.1 ha area delineated by the paired transect lines. After the herbaceous sampling is completed at each plot, all tree seedlings and saplings in the 10 m² plot are identified to species and assigned to one of three size classes: (1) seedlings – stems < 0.5m tall, (2) small saplings – stems ≥ 0.5m tall but < 2.5cm diameter at breast height (dbh) and (3) large saplings – stems ≥ 2.5cm dbh but < 5.0cm dbh. Either standard dbh tapes or electronic calipers can be used to measure dbh.

After the seedling and sapling data have been collected, the transect lines are left on the ground and the internal rectangular 0.1 ha area delineated by the paired transect lines is surveyed for all trees ≥ 5.0cm dbh. Each tree is recorded by species on a field data sheet. For each tree, the dbh to the nearest 0.1cm is determined. Each tree is also assigned a condition code (L= live or D = dead) for use in structural analysis. Additionally, each tree receives a crown position code (1 -5) which indicates the canopy position of each overstory tree. The tree data will be used to understand succession and stand development. Refer to SOP #8 "Conducting the Woody Species Sampling" for additional details on collecting tree species data.

Processing Unknown Plant Species

Plants not immediately identified in the plot are collected and recorded on the data sheet with an unknown specimen code (<park code> <unknown number> <date>, e.g., WICRunk2_7_03). If at least 10 – 15 individuals of the unknown species are present at a site, a specimen is collected outside the plot and placed in a plant press for later examination. A small or partial specimen is kept in a field notebook with the description and unknown code to insure consistent application of unknown codes among sampling units. Location, description and habitat information are recorded using an unknown specimen data sheet. If a specimen cannot be found outside the plot or the plant is rare, a description and location in the plot are recorded.

Collected material is mounted on acid-free herbarium paper, kept in insect proof containers and becomes reference specimens. Rare, threatened, or endangered species are not collected. Reference specimens are housed in the herbarium at Wilson's Creek National Battlefield. The U.S. Department of Agriculture, Natural Resources Conservation Service's Plant List of Accepted Nomenclature, Taxonomy and Symbols (PLANTS) database (USDA, NRCS 2004) is used to standardize plant taxonomy.

Data Management

Effective data management allows the project leader to store and retrieve large quantities of data securely and efficiently. Data management typically becomes an issue when sample sizes are in the range of 10^4 to 10^5 or greater. Natural resource monitoring databases will frequently exceed these values. Database design should accommodate these sample sizes while meeting project requirements.

Overview of Database Design

Monitoring databases share many similarities with data warehouses. They emphasize events that are stored in one or more core tables. These event tables, in turn, are linked to parameter tables that provide the information necessary to understand the events. The NPS Inventory and Monitoring Program developed the natural resource database template (NRDT) as a proof-of-concept database model for managing long-term ecological monitoring data (http://science.nature.nps.gov/im/apps/template). The NRDT is an event-based design that standardizes the relationship between location, time and event data. The template promotes the integration of Inventory and Monitoring datasets. It also improves development efficiency by encouraging the reuse of design features.

The database used for vegetation community monitoring is called VEGMON. Like other natural resource monitoring databases, observation events in VEGMON form the center of the database. Events include observations for species frequency or percent cover, recruitment of young tree species and percent canopy cover. VEGMON observations reference parameter tables such as plant species, cover classes, plant guilds and tree conditions.

Data Entry

A number of features have been designed into VEGMON to minimize errors during the data entry process. The user interface helps to create a logical relationship between field datasheets and database records. Standardized identifiers for sample location and time are selected from choices provided by the user interface. Species and plot sizes are selected from lists linked to appropriate reference tables. Other fields contain project-specific data and prohibit entry of values not included in reference tables. Consequently, only valid names or measures may be entered and spelling mistakes are eliminated.

Data Verification and Validation

Data verification immediately follows data entry and involves checking computerized records against the original source, usually paper field records. Once the computerized data are verified as accurately reflecting the original field data, the paper forms are archived and the electronic version is used for all subsequent data activities.

Data validation involves checking the accuracy of data against independent controls or specifications. There are three types of data validation used in VEGMON. They are:

- Referential integrity
- Limited lists for nominal data
- Reasonable values for continuous data

Referential integrity is typically built into the database design by way of table relationships and their key fields that have data constraints such as "unique" and "no null". Nominal data can be controlled by a user interface containing choice values that are limited to lists. The resulting data can be validated using a "SELECT DISTINCT" query. Validation of continuous data is more challenging and more complex. It requires an understanding of the nature of the data (e.g., the sampling design and how the parameters were measured). This knowledge is necessary to identify the normal range of continuous data and which outlier values truly represent errors. Details regarding data management activities are located in SOP #11 "Data Management."

Staff Roles and Responsibilities

Staff roles and responsibilities overlap between project leader and data manager. The project leader is primarily responsible for data quality. The project leader must ensure data quality throughout the process of data entry, data verification and data validation. The data manager may assist by identifying or implementing validation methods that will reduce the risk of error. The data manager's primary role is to assure functionality of database applications prior to and during data processing. Finally and most importantly, the database manager is also responsible for secure backups of all project data.

Analysis and Reporting

A critical component of any long-term monitoring protocol is a consistent and systematic way of analyzing and reporting on information (data) collected. Further, the information must serve two purposes: to describe the current condition, or status, of a plant community; and be robust enough to detect community changes through time. The plant community variables and indices selected for data summary purposes are complete, descriptive and easily interpretable. Summary indices and variables will provide information to park managers on the status of the target communities and, coupled with ground-level cover data, provide feedback on the effects of implemented management efforts (e.g., restoration efforts or disturbance regime).

Section I of SOP #12 "Data Summary and Analysis" gives step-by-step details on how to: 1) determine species abundance, richness, diversity and evenness, 2) estimate abundance of prairie plant guilds, 3) calculate core species and optimized frequency and 4) calculate woody species basal area, density and regeneration class data. All calculations are made at the site level, so means and standard deviations can be calculated for each study unit or for park wide inferences. These parameters should be analyzed each time a survey is completed.

Vegetation Data Analysis

Many variables collected in vegetation community monitoring are spatially and temporally dynamic, yet serve an important purpose in providing descriptive information about the communities monitored. Community composition describes the spatial distribution of plants through the use of basic measurements – frequency and foliar cover. From these variables other important ecological measures (indices or metrics) are determined. These variables and indices are the basis for assessing changes in vegetation communities through time. A more detailed description of these variables can be found in Section I of SOP #12 "Data Summary and Analysis."

An underlying purpose of the HTLN is to design and implement long-term ecological monitoring to evaluate the integrity of park natural resources and contribute to the evaluation of park management objectives and goals. The approach towards long-term analysis of monitoring data is therefore critical to meet this goal. A subset of the variables is selected for specific analyses relative to park vegetation communities and management objectives. The focus is on temporal and spatial change in community composition and structure and how it is related to environmental and management measurements. Analyses for community change detection begin with relatively simple approaches (exploratory analyses, parameter estimation and control charts) and progress to more complicated analyses when biologically important changes seem to be occurring and the simpler analyses do not yield all the necessary information.
Section II of SOP #12 "Data Summary and Analysis" contains more details on constructing controls charts and conducting trends analysis.

Reporting

To facilitate timely dissemination of monitoring results, status reports should be completed by May 1 of the year following data collection. Baseline status reports will be prepared after the first year a park or community has been sampled. More extensive summary reports, including trend analysis, should be completed for those parks with at least four sampling years after every sampling event depending on the rate of change in the vegetation community dynamics and the need for summary information to guide resource management. Refer to SOP #13 "Reporting and Presentation" for details on report structure and style.

Report formats will follow the established and most current format of the NRTR style. Each report will be assigned a TIC number and be made available in electronic format on the HTLN website (http://science.nature.nps.gov/im/units/htln)

Personnel Requirements and Training

Roles and Responsibilities
The project manager is the lead ecologist for implementing the vegetation community monitoring protocol and is supervised by the program coordinator for the HTLN Program. Because of the need for a high level of consistency in implementing the protocol, the project manager will be responsible for training the seasonal and permanent personnel assisting with the monitoring efforts.

Qualifications and Training
A competent, detail-oriented observer is essential for collecting credible, high-quality data in vegetation communities. Observer bias in the estimation of cover and mis-identification of species will affect the ability to detect valid trends or changes in vegetation communities through time (Elzinga *et al*. 1998). Field observers must be proficient at accurately identifying plants and estimating plant coverage. Observers should also have good organizational skills, memory retention and an ability to work methodically and consistently under difficult conditions.

Training is essential for developing competent observers. Herbarium specimens and comparative notes on difficult or uncommon species should be provided for field observers. Observers should be tested frequently on their ability to identify plant species, tailoring the testing for the more problematic look-alike species. Time should also be invested in training personnel on cover estimation. Estimating cover is best taught at the start of the season in the field with all crew members present and then reviewed periodically throughout the summer to reduce within-year observer differences in cover estimation. Observers should familiarize themselves with the HTLN standard cover classes and vegetation guilds described in SOP #5 "Measuring Frequency and Cover of Herbaceous and Shrub Species." Prior to the field season, observers should practice estimating cover of different vegetation guilds and ground cover categories using practice plots. Differences in cover estimation between observers will strongly affect survey results. Refer to SOP #2, "Training Observers" to review techniques helpful in training observers in both plant identification and cover estimation.

Operational Requirements

Annual Workload and Field Schedule
Monitoring will require at minimum a four-person crew each year. Field person days will be dependent upon the parks sampled, logistics, weather and crew skill level. For example, in 2008, 85 sites were sampled in five parks in 108 field person days.

Facility and Equipment Needs

The nature of vegetation monitoring work does not require special facilities beyond normal office space and equipment and herbarium storage. A list of field equipment needs for one crew can be found SOP #1, "Preparations and Equipment Setup Prior to the Field Season." If two or more crews work simultaneously, equipment requirements will increase accordingly.

Budget Considerations

Approximately seven days, including travel, are required to complete the sampling for each park group. Personnel expenses for field work are based on a crew of four people, an ecologist, a botanist and two seasonal biological science technicians. Field costs will vary from year to year depending on the skill level and size of the crew (Table 4). Data management personnel expenses include staff time of biological science technicians, project manager and data manager. Costs include the purchase of equipment and supplies listed in SOP #1 as well as maintenance and or replacement of equipment shared among multiple projects (e.g. GPS units, cameras, vehicles).

Table 4. Estimated annual budget for vegetation community monitoring by the Heartland Inventory and Monitoring Network.

Category	Cost
Staff salary	$156,885
Admin support to WICR	$4,032
Field work travel	$5,776
Computer hardware and software	$1,520
Vehicle lease	$3,648
Field and office equipment	$2,736
Supplies	$1,824
TOTAL	**$176,421**

Procedures for Revising the Protocol

Over time, revisions to the protocol narrative and to SOPs are to be expected. Careful documentation of changes to the protocol and a library of previous protocol versions are essential for maintaining consistency in data collection and for appropriate treatment of the data during data summary and analysis. The Microsoft Access® database for each monitoring component contains a field that identifies which version of the protocol was being used when the data were collected.

The rationale for dividing a sampling protocol into a protocol narrative with supporting SOPs is based on the following:

1. The protocol narrative is a general overview of the protocol giving the history and justification for the work and an overview of the sampling methods, but does not provide all the methodological details. The protocol narrative will only be revised if major changes are made to the protocol.

2. The SOPs, in contrast, are very specific step-by-step instructions for performing a given task. They are expected to be revised more frequently than the protocol narrative.

3.   When a SOP is revised, in most cases, it is not necessary to revise the protocol narrative to reflect the specific changes made to the SOP.

4.   All versions of the protocol narrative and SOPs will be archived in a protocol library.

The steps for changing the protocol (either the protocol narrative or the SOPs) are outlined in SOP #14, "Revising the Protocol." Each SOP contains a revision history log that should be filled out each time a SOP is revised to explain why the change was made and to assign a new version number to the revised SOP. The new version of the SOP and/or protocol narrative should then be archived in the HTLN protocol library under the appropriate folder.

Literature Cited

Beers, T.W., P.E. Dress and L.C. Wensel. 1966. Aspect transformation in site productivity research. Journal of Forestry 64:691-692.

Bragg, T.B. 1995. The physical environment of Great Plains grasslands. In A. Joern and K.H. Keeler, editors. The Changing Prairie. Oxford: Oxford University Press.

Collins, S.L. 1987. Interaction of disturbances in tallgrass prairie: a field experiment. Ecology 68: 1243 – 1250.

Collins, S.L. 1992. Fire frequency and community heterogeneity in tallgrass prairie vegetation. Ecology 73(6): 2001 – 2006.

Collins, S.L. 2000. Disturbance frequency and community stability in native tallgrass prairie. The American Naturalist 155 (3): 311 – 325.

Collins, S.L. and S.M. Glenn. 1991. Importance of spatial and temporal dynamics in species regional abundance and distribution. Ecology 72: 654 – 664.

Collins, S.L. and S.M. Glenn. 1997. Intermediate disturbance and its relationship to within- and between-patch dynamics. New Zealand Journal of Ecology 21: 103 – 110.

Daubenmire, R.F. 1959. Canopy coverage method of vegetation analysis. Northwest Science 33: 43 – 64.

Davison, C. and K. Kindscher. 1999. Tools for diversity: fire, grazing and mowing on tallgrass prairies. Ecological Restoration 17 (3): 136 – 143.

DeBacker, M.D., A.N. Sasseen, C. Becker, G.A. Rowell, L.P. Thomas, J.R. Boetsch and G.D. Wilson. 2004. Vegetation Community Monitoring Protocol for the Heartland I&M Network and Prairie Cluster Prototype Monitoring Program. National Park Service, Heartland Inventory and Monitoring Network and Prairie Cluster Prototype Monitoring Program, Wilson's Creek National Battlefield, Republic, Missouri. 40p. plus appendices.

DeBacker, M.D., C.C. Young (editor), P. Adams, L. Morrison, D. Peitz, G.A. Rowell and M. Williams and D. Bowles 2005. Heartland I&M Network and Prairie Cluster Prototype Monitoring Program Vital Signs Monitoring Plan. NPS, Heartland I&M Network and Prairie Cluster Prototype Monitoring Program, Wilson's Creek National Battlefield, Republic, Missouri. 104 p. plus appendices.

Earnest, S.K.M. and J.H. Brown. 2001. Homeostasis and compensation: the role of species and resources in ecosystem stability. Ecology 82 (8): 2118 – 2132.

Elzinga, C.L., D.W. Salzer and J.W. Willoughby. 1998. Measuring and Monitoring Plant Populations. BLM Technical Reference 1730 – 1. Denver, Colorado.

Eyre, F.H. 1980. Forest Cover Types of the United States and Canada. Society of American Foresters, Washington, D.C., 148pp.

Fuhlendorf, S.D. and D.M. Engle. 2001. Restoring heterogeneity on rangelands: ecosystem management based on evolutionary grazing patterns. BioScience 51 (8): 625 – 632.

Gibson, D.J. 1988. Regeneration and fluctuations of tallgrass prairie vegetation in response to burning frequency. Bulletin of the Torrey Botanical Club 115:1-12.

Glenn, S.M. and S.L. Collins. 1992. Effects of scale and disturbance on rates of immigration and extinction of species in prairies. Oikos 63(2):273-280.

Greig-Smith, P. 1983. Quantitative Plant Ecology. Berkeley, California: University of California Press.

Howe, H. 1999. Dominance, diversity and grazing in tallgrass restoration. Ecological Restoration 17 (1 and 2): 59 – 66.

Johnson, P.S., S.R. Shifley and R. Rogers. 2002.   The ecology and silvicul ture of oaks. CABI, New York, 503pp.

Knapp, A.K. and T.R. Seastedt. 1998. Introduction: grasslands, Konza Prairie and long-term ecological research. In A.K. Knapp, J.M. Briggs, D.C. Harnett and S.L. Collins, editors. Grassland dynamics: long-term ecological research in tallgrass prairie. Oxford: Oxford University Press.

Knapp, A.K., J.M. Blair, J.M. Briggs, S.L. Collins, D.C. Hartnett, L.C. Johnson and E.G. Towne. 1999. The keystone role of bison in North American tallgrass prairie. BioScience 49: 39 – 50.

Knopf, F.L. and F.B. Samson. 1997. Conservation of grassland vertebrates. In F.L. Knopf and F.B. Samson, editors. Ecology and Conservation of Great Plains Vertebrates. New York, New York: Springer-Verlag.

Lesica, P. and B.M. Steele. 1996. A method for monitoring long-term population trends: an example using rare arctic-alpine plants. Ecological Applications 6 (3): 879 – 887.

McShea, W.J. and W.M. Healy. 2002. Oak Forest Ecosystems: Ecology and Management for Wildlife. The Johns Hopkins University Press, Baltimore, 432pp.

Nelson, P.W. 2005. The Terrestrial Natural Communities of Missouri, revised edition. Missouri Natural Areas Committee, 550pp.

Oliver, C.D. and B.C. Larson. 1996. Forest Stand Dynamics, updated edition. John Wiley and Sons, Inc., New York, 520pp.

Peet, R.K., T.R. Wentworth and P.S. White. 1998. A flexible, multipurpose method for recording vegetation composition and structure. Castanea 63(3):262-274.

Peitz, D.G., G.A. Rowell, J.L. Haack, K.M. James, L.W. Morrison and M.D. DeBacker. 2008. Breeding Bird Monitoring Protocol for the Heartland Network Inventory and Monitoring Program. Natural Resource Report NPS/HTLN/NRR- 2008/044. National Park Service, Fort Collins, Colorado.

Thompson, S.K. 1992. Sampling. Wiley Publishing, New York, NY, 343pp.

USDA, NRCS. 2004. The PLANTS Database, Version 3.5 (http://plants.usda.gov). National Plant Data Center, Baton Rouge, LA 70874-4490 USA.

USDS, National Park Service. 2003. Fire Monitoring Handbook. Boise (ID): Fire Management Program Center, National Interagency Fire Center. 274p.

Standard Operating Procedures

Vegetation Community Monitoring Protocol
for the Heartland Inventory and Monitoring Network

Standard Operating Procedure 1: Preparations and Equipment Setup Prior to the Field Season

Version 2.00 (June 2009)

Revision History Log:

Previous Version #	Revision Date	Author	Changes Made	Reason for Change	New Version #
1.00	6/19/2009	K.M. James	Minor edits to entire document	Change to the revisit design	2.00

This SOP provides information to prepare for the summer field season, including a list of field equipment needed. It also provides information for constructing sampling frames used in plant community sampling. Finally, this SOP provides descriptions of data sheets used during sampling, guidelines for the numbers of copies that are necessary for each sampling trip and example data sheets.

I.   General Preparations

Prior to the field season each year, usually beginning in March or April, all observers should review the entire protocol, including SOPs. Refreshing plant identification skills is particularly important, as is reviewing the standard sampling procedures implemented at each plot. The following list includes key points to consider in preparing for the upcoming field season.

A field notebook for the survey year should be prepared with pages for entry of sampling schedules, observer names, field hours and unique happenings that may influence how the data are reported. Information included in trip reports is based on what is recorded in field notebooks so it is imperative that they are clearly organized for ease of field note entry.

Species lists from previous years as well as pressed plant specimens should be reviewed if available to identify any unique plants that may be encountered. Prior knowledge of species most likely to be encountered in a park will aid botanists in preparing for the sampling season. Therefore, species lists from previous community monitoring efforts in a park or site should be compiled and compared to reference manuals to identify species not recorded which have a probability of being recorded. Copies of these combined species list should be carried into the field as quick references.

Plant community monitoring will begin no sooner than mid-May and extend no later than the end of July, a period that coincides with the growing season across the Great Plains. Inclement weather and personnel workloads will preclude the scheduling of sampling events to specific annual dates. Sampling dates should be scheduled and logistics organized prior to the start of each field season.

Monitoring efforts throughout a summer will require a four-person crew (two people to sample and two to record data) approximately five to ten field days to complete one sampling trip. A single trip may contain two to three different parks.

An equipment list should be compiled and equipment organized and made ready for the field season several weeks prior to the first sampling trip. This allows time to make needed repairs and order equipment. The following is a list of field equipment needs for one crew; if two or more crews work simultaneously, equipment needs will change accordingly (Table 1.1).

II.   Construction of Sampling Frames

Vegetation Sampling Frame

The vegetation sampling frame uses sixteen to seventeen flexible tent poles that are joined together (the number of poles necessary is dependent on the thickness and length of the tent poles used) with ten yards of elastic (1/8 inch in diameter) that is threaded through the poles. This keeps the tent poles completely together except in one spot, so that frame can be broken down and easily carried or stored. Two ropes (3.5 m in length) are attached to the frame by using small hose clamps and key rings. The clamps holding the ropes are spaced 2.8 m apart. The ropes are for dividing the 10 m² circle into four equal quarter sections (Figure 1.1).

The frame is easily disassembled and can be neatly packed for travel to and from parks. Further, the frame can be quickly assembled and disassembled in the field once reaching a site. This accommodates foot travel between sites. Because the sampling frame is cumbersome and bulky once fully expanded, it is best to assemble the frame as close to the site as possible. Ideally, a minimum of three sampling frames in excellent working condition should be available throughout the summer; one is kept in the vehicle and two are in the field with the crew.

Using tent poles for the outer frame is beneficial during sampling because it provides a visible boundary of the 10 m^2 plot and allows greater precision in abundance estimates. The 10 m^2 plot is divided into quarters by ropes to facilitate accurate estimates of foliar cover for each species. In tall thick vegetation the tent pole frame may not be strong enough to get through the vegetation. In this case a frame made of metal bars and 1 inch black PVC tubing should be used. In wooded areas or difficult terrain, the tent pole frame can be too cumbersome to maneuver and the red and white sampling pins and rope must be used to construct the 10 m^2 plot. This sampling frame should only be used when absolutely necessary because the four pins in the "corners" of the circle provide the only reference to the perimeter of the plot.

To assemble the frame in the field, first unravel the ropes around the tent poles. Second, starting with one of the end poles connect the poles together until they are all attached and form a circle. Lastly, make sure the ropes are not twisted together; if they are twisted, unhook one of the key rings and untwist it. It is important to prevent mud from getting lodged in the metal part of the tent poles, which can cause the poles to crack.

Table 1.1. Equipment needs associated with vegetation community sampling

Activity Equipm	ent
Plot Establishment and Set-Up	<ul><li>GPS units (2)</li><li>Compass (2)</li><li>Data sheets for site establishment</li><li>Digital Camera</li><li>Flagging – for marking rebar and witness trees and keeping field equipment visible</li><li>Sampling frames (3) – the 10 m^2 frames</li><li>Hoops – function as the nested plots within the 10 m^2 frames<ul><li>1 m^2 (4)</li><li>0.1 m^2 (4)</li><li>0.01 m^2 (4)</li></ul></li><li>Maps</li><li>Metal detector – for finding transect ends</li><li>Rebar and hammer</li><li>50 meter Tapes (4)</li><li>Yellow Caps – fit over the ends of each rebar to increase rebar visibility</li><li>Pliers/Leatherman</li><li>Tags and Wire</li></ul>
Data collection	<ul><li>Data sheets</li><li>Clip boards</li><li>Pencils</li><li>Unknown Specimen Book</li><li>Unknown Specimen Forms</li><li>Write-In-Rain Paper</li><li>Species Identification Manuals and Taxonomical Books</li><li>Plant Press</li><li>Handlens</li></ul>
Additional equipment used when sampling wooded communities	<ul><li>DBH tapes</li><li>Calipers</li><li>Densiometer</li><li>Ropes and stakes</li></ul>

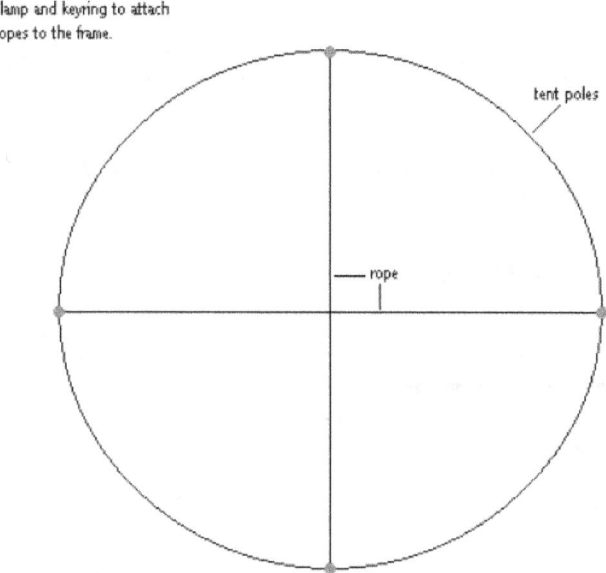

Clamp and keyring to attach
ropes to the frame.

tent poles

rope

Figure 1.1. Sampling frame.

Nested Plot Frames

The nested circular plots are of the following area measurements: 1.0 m², 0.1 m² and 0.01 m².
They are made of hollow PVC tubes and are held together by PVC threaded connectors. Table
1.2 lists the dimensions necessary for the construction of each circular frame. Each frame is
formed into a circle, joined with a connector. For the 0.01 m² nested plot a large metal hose
clamp can be used, instead of a PVC tube. Throughout the summer, a minimum of four frames
for each nested plot size in good working condition are a necessity.

Table 1.2. Nested circular plot dimensions.

Plot size Le	ngth of PVC tube	Additional tools
1 m²	3.54 m	PVC connector
0.1 m²	1.12 m	PVC connector
0.01 m² 0.3	5 m	PVC connector

III.   Field Data Forms

The following field data forms are used in sampling. Details on filling out the data sheets are
described in the corresponding SOP. Most datasheets are specific to each location, but with a
similar format. Approximately twenty-five percent of the field data forms should be copied to
write-in-the-rain paper.

Vegetation Data Field Forms Used at All Sample Units
1. **Site Establishment Data Sheet for Plant Community Monitoring** (Appendix 1.1, Data
   Form 1) – this data sheet is filled out during the initial establishment of a site. It is not

26

necessary to complete this data sheet on subsequent return visits. See SOP #4 "Establishing and Marking Permanent Sample Sites" for details.

2. **Herbaceous Data Collection Form** (Appendix 1.1, Data Form 2) – this set of data sheets is filled out during each sampling visit to a particular site. Prior to sampling a park, the species data from previous years are used to generate a plot-specific species list that is incorporated into the data sheet. For each transect, a set of five species data sheets is generated – one for each 10 m^2 plot along the transect. Therefore, each site requires two sets of species data sheets, one for each transect. Special attention must be made to verify that the plot number being sampled matches the plot number on the data sheet prior to collecting data. Data collected within the 10 m^2 plot include herbaceous and shrubby vegetation, woody seedlings and saplings and canopy cover in wooded areas. Information gathered in the nested plots is also recorded on these data sheets. See SOP #5 "Measuring Frequency and Cover of Herbaceous and Shrub Species", SOP #7 "Measuring Ground Cover" and SOP #8 "Conducting the Woody Species Sampling" for details.

3. **Unknown Data Sheet** (Appendix 1.1, Data Form 3) – this form is used when a plant specimen unfamiliar to the sampling crew is encountered. The information serves as a detailed written description of the unknown specimen and contains a unique code used to identify the unknown specimen. For each unknown specimen collected, there is one form that is filled out during the initial recording and collection. The unique code given to the specimen is immediately transcribed into the Unknown Specimen Book. If the plant is re-encountered, the initial unknown specimen form and book are referred to and the unique unknown code used in lieu of a species code. See SOP #5, "Measuring Frequency and Cover of Herbaceous Shrub Species" for details.

Vegetation data field forms specific to wooded habitats
4. **Woody Species Overstory and Understory Data Collection Form** – (Appendix 1.1, Data Form 4) this data sheet is used to collect data in wooded communities where woody species greater than 5.0 cm diameter at breast height (dbh) are present. One data sheet is required for each site. See SOP #8, "Conducting the Woody Species Sampling" for details.

Appendix 1.1. Example Data Sheets

Data Form 1 – Site Establishment Sheet for Plant Community Monitoring

Park _____ Primary sampling unit _____ Site number _____ Pasture/unit _____

Establishment date _____ Established by _____ _____

Soil series / site selection information _____

Azimuth of transects (from 0 to 50m) _____ Monumenting: GPS only   Witness markers

Monumenting notes _____

Slope angle (%): Start _____ Finish_____ Slope aspect (degrees): Start _____ Center _____ Finish _____
(from A line to B line; indicate + or -)   (from A line to B line)

Terrain shape: downslope _____ +90° (right) _____ +180° (upslope) _____ +270° (left) _____
(15 m from site center, angle in %; indicate + or -)

Topographic position: level   lower-slope   mid-slope   upper-slope   crest   ledge   depression   draw

Hydrologic regime: permanently flooded   semi-permanently flooded   seasonally/temporarily flooded

           intermittently flooded   seep   upland

Surface water: in plot   <50m   >50m

Vegetation type: upland prairie   riparian woodland   rocky site   other: _____

Data Form 2 – Herbaceous Data Collection Form, Plot specific example form for EFMO including canopy cover (densiometer), seedling and sapling data collection

EFMO_VegMon_1   10A

Date: _____

Collectors ini: _____

Densiometer readings: _____, _____, _____, _____

Start time: _____

End time: _____

Data entered (ini): _____

Verified (ini): _____

Species	.01	.1	1	10	cover
bare soil					
bare rock					
grass litter					
leaf litter					
woody debris					
unvegetated					

Plot	Cumulative Species List
10A	AMORPHA CANESCENS
10A	AMPHICARPA BRACTEATA
10A	ARALIA RACEMOSA
10A	BAPTISIA BRACTEATA VAR. LEUCOPHAEA
10A	BROMUS PUBESCENS
10A	CAREX SPP
10A	CIRCAEA LUTETIANA SSP. CANADENSIS
10A	DESMODIUM GLUTINOSUM
10A	DESMODIUM NUDIFLORUM
10A	FRAGARIA VIRGINIANA
10A	HELIANTHUS STRUMOSUS
10A	LAPORTEA CANADENSIS
10A	MAIANTHEMUM RACEMOSUM SSP. RACEMOSUM
10A	MUHLENBERGIA TENUIFLORA
10A	POLYGONATUM BIFLORUM
10A	PTERIDIUM AQUILINUM
10A	RUBUS SPP
10A	SMILAX TAMNOIDES
10A	SOLIDAGO ULMIFOLIA
10A	TARAXACUM OFFICINALE
10A	TOXICODENDRON RADICANS
10A	VITIS SPP
10A	ZANTHOXYLUM AMERICANUM

Species	Seedling	Small Sap	Lrg Sap

Seedling (<0.5 m tall)
Small Sapling (>or= 0.5 m tall, < 2.5 cm dbh)
Lrg Sapling (>or= 2.5 cm dbh, < 5.0 cm dbh)

Data Form 3 – Unknown Data Sheet

Park:_____   Unknown   Code:_____
Transect & Plot:_____
Date:_____
Plant Type & General Description: herb   shrub   tree   vine   grass   sedge other_____

Most salient feature:

Leaf Characteristics:
          Leaf Type: (cmpd/simple, arrangement, etc.)

          Margin:

          Other: (pubescence, sap, stipules, etc)

Stem Characteristics: (shape, pubescence, bud)

Flower Characteristics: (color, location, floral formula)

General and Microhabitat Characteristics:

Collected: Yes   No

Best Guess:

Confirmed to be:

Data Form 4 – Woody Species Overstory Data Collection Form, Example form for Effigy Mounds National Monument, Iowa.

Overstory Measurement at EFMO

Transect #
Date:
Collectors:

Trees > 5cm dbh

Species:	DBH	Condition	CPC	Is coppice (Y/N)

Standard Operating Procedure 2: Training Observers

Version 1.00 (December 2004)

Revision History Log:

Previous Version #	Revision Date	Author	Changes Made	Reason for Change	New Version #

This Standard Operating Procedure explains the preferred training procedures for all vegetation monitoring crew members. Pre-season and during-season procedures are described. Training procedures are in place to promote the following: (1) the identification of plants in both vegetative form and in flower; and (2) consistent estimates of foliar cover. Details on standardizing plant identification for problematic plants and foliar cover estimates are provided.

I.   Training Observers in Plant Identification

Field botany differs from taxonomy in that field identification must often rely on vegetative characteristics. Hired observers are expected to be familiar with the differences in terminology and definitions for vegetative characteristics, as well as be trained in plant taxonomy.

Suggestions for training field botanists are listed below:
1.   Provide a plant species list including all plant species likely to be encountered throughout the summer to all crew members prior to the first tour.

2.   Prior to the start of the field season, all field botanists should be encouraged to:
   a. Review notes in field plant identification and taxonomy.
   b. Practice plant identification skills and make use of herbarium specimens when possible.
   c. Regardless of skill level, spend time in the field to become familiar with the plants on the species list prior to the initiation of summer sampling.
   d. Obtain a plant taxonomy guide and begin to attach descriptive terms utilized taxonomically in describing plant characteristics to what you are observing in the field.

3.   Focus field botany training efforts on species-level information rather than on formal taxonomy.

4.   Provide standardized species lists that list the key vegetative characteristics used in field identification. Descriptions that list the specific differences between look-alike species standardize identifications among personnel and serve as communication tools among the field botanists and the crew leader. Further, because descriptive lists are improved upon each year utilizing the advances made by the crew, they can serve as motivational tools as well as learning tools.

5.   Before each sampling trip during the field season, all field botanists should be instructed to:
     a.   Review the park-specific and plot-specific species lists
     b.   Read through field notes collected on problem species and the unknown records in the field notebook.
     c.   Study herbarium specimens and problem species keys in preparation for the upcoming trip.

6.   Conduct review sessions throughout the summer. Incorporate challenging plant identification quizzes into the session for testing purposes and motivation. Review species identification of known difficult and problem species and those that are suggested by the crew. Sessions are most successful when viewed as a relaxed but challenging experience and can serve to correct misidentifications.

7.   There are numerous reference materials that are useful plant identification guides and references. Providing copies for perusal and study throughout the summer strengthens plant identification. Major references include:
     •   McGregor, R.L., T.M. Barkley, R.E. Brooks and E.K. Schofield. 1986. Flora of the Great Plains. University Press of Kansas: Lawrence, Kansas.
     •   Harris, J.G. and M.W. Harris. 1994. Plant Identification Terminology: An illustrated Glossary. Spring Lake Publishing: Payson, Utah.
     •   Steyermark, J.A. 1963. Flora of Missouri. Iowa State University Press: Ames, Iowa.

II.   Training Observers in Estimating Foliar Cover

Estimations of foliar cover can provide a picture of the abundance of a species relative to that of others within the vegetation community. Training observers to collectively provide estimates that are accurate and precise is challenging. Clear communication among the crew members, particularly between crew members and the crew leader, will ensure that all are in agreement on how and what to estimate. The challenge in training observers in estimation is to reduce the variability among all estimates obtained in the field, thus reducing the sampling error rate.

1.   At the start of the field season, train observers on cover estimation in a group setting. All crew members must be in agreement for what constitutes a specific coverage; cover estimation should not be a one-person decision.

2.   Encourage both seasoned and new field personnel to memorize the specific cover class breakdown and codes used for the HTLN vegetation monitoring project. Because there

are numerous cover class breakdowns utilized by different monitoring projects, often experienced botanists will find it difficult to break away from past cover class breaks. Alternatively, cover class codes are often difficult to remember for new field botanists.

3. Reiterate the importance of obtaining both an accurate estimation and a high level of precision around an estimate. When training new observers, demonstrating what constitutes 15% of a plot for a bunch grass species versus a broad-leaved forb is as important as discussing how to do so. Utilize the collective knowledge of seasoned field botanists, emphasizing the importance of sharing their experiences with the crew. Communication among the experienced and new observers will ensure a higher degree of precision in foliar cover estimations.

4. Provide a half day of training in various habitats when training new observers; provide two to three hours of training with the entire crew in various habitats to acquire consistency among all observers.

5. Throughout the sampling season, re-train field sampling crews in cover estimation. Periodically test all crew members in species identification and in cover class estimates.

6. Recalibrate the field crew to one another every few weeks throughout the summer. This can be done by shuffling around observer pairs, or by taking a few moments together as a group.

Vegetation Community Monitoring Protocol
For the Heartland Inventory and Monitoring Network

Standard Operating Procedure 3: Using the Global Positioning System

Version 2.00 (June 2009)

Revision History Log:

Prev. Version #	Revision Date	Author	Changes Made	Reason for Change	New Version #
1.00 6/19/09		J.L. Haack	Entire document	Focus on operational use of GPS in project	2.00

This SOP describes the procedures for collecting and navigating to vegetation community site locations. For specifics on how to use the HTLN GPS units, please see the document: Heartland Network Operational Plan for GPS.

I.   Location Site Establishment

When establishing a new vegetation community site it is important to spatially record the most accurate location possible. Whenever possible, use a mapping grade GPS unit with an antenna that reduces multipath. For each site the transect endpoint, marked by a piece of rebar (in some cases this may be a nail-in or anchor), is the location that will be collected with the GPS unit.

The following settings should be applied to the GPS unit:
- System: UTM
- Datum: NAD 1983 (conus) CORS96
- Zone (is park dependent):
  o Zone 14N : HOME, PIPE and TAPR
  o Zone 15N: EFMO, GWCA, HEHO, HOSP, PERI and WICR
- Altitude Measure: Height Above Ellipsoid (HAE)
- Units: Meters
- Antenna Height: Is dependent on who is collecting data. No matter if the antenna is internal or external the measurement should be set for the collection person. Measure the distance from the bottom of the antenna to the ground with a meter tape and enter the measurement in the GPS antenna height settings.
- PDOP: Should not be greater than 6.0 (the lower the number the more accurate the location)
- GPS Correction: None or Use Uncorrected (because data will be post-processed differentially corrected later)
- Satellite Elevation: Minimum of 15 degrees.

To start data collection first you must name the GPS rover file. For data management reasons, name the GPS rover file being collected with the park code, the year of collection and 'veg' (ex: wicrveg2009 or peri2009veg). In the rover file name, do not include spaces. All points that are collected for a park can be saved within the same rover file unless more than 5 days has elapsed since the start of data collection. If this has occurred, create a new rover file with the same name, but with a B, C, 2, etc. at the end.

Sites will only be collected as point features. For each point a minimum of **50** positions should be collected at a **1 second** interval. While the positions are being acquired hold the antenna still over the rebar or marker being collected. If the antenna is moved or shifted during collection, which decreases accuracy, please recollect the point. The points themselves should be named with their transect code. The transect code is the site number followed by AS, AF, BS, or BF. The letter represents the transect line A or B, as well as the transect end S for start and F for finish.

Once the site data have been collected, return the GPS unit to the GIS specialist for data processing.

II.   Site Navigation

For site navigation the same GPS unit settings used for site establishment can be used, with one exception. This exception is GPS Correction, which can be set to real-time correction. Real-time correction may improve the accuracy of the GPS unit and at times may be called WAAS or SBAS.

Before going out into the field the GPS unit should be loaded with the waypoints needed for the sites being visited. Once in the field the first thing to do is turn the GPS unit on (and if needed open the spatial software program) and set it in the open where no harm will come to it, so it has time to lock into satellites. After navigating to a site double check that the transect tag matches the waypoint and map label. If they do not match, the transect tag is the correct one. Please make a note of the mismatch and inform the GIS specialist of the discrepancy.

When using a HTLN mapping grade GPS unit to navigate back to a site, expect the unit to get you within 2 m of the site. If you choose to use a recreational grade GPS unit, expect to be within 5 to 30 m of the site.

III.   Notes

When not using the GPS unit for more than 2 minutes, turn the unit off to save battery power. Make sure to close all software programs first before turning the GPS unit off. When the GPS is not being used, place the unit in an area out of harm's way and not in direct sunlight. Each GPS unit has a different battery life, look up what the life is for the unit you take out.

There may be times when the GPS unit will not give you a reading. The first thing to do is check the GPS plan to see if it is just a bad time of day, due to the arrangement of the GPS satellites. If it is one of these times, the only thing to do is be patient and wait, this should correct itself in less than an hour. It is wise to check the GPS plan before leaving for the field, so this does not cause delays. Another reason for no GPS reading is the GPS receiver is being blocked. Make sure your hand or other equipment is not blocking the receiver. At other times a tree or hill can block part of the horizon making it impossible for the GPS satellites signal to reach you. If you are collecting data, you will need to offset to collect your data. Go to an area where a GPS signal can be collect and offset back to the site by using a compass and rangefinder/meter tape. However, if you are navigating also go to where a signal can be received and then guide the other members of your crew to the site location.

Please be familiar with the Heartland Network Operational Plan for GPS before going into the field. There should be a copy in each HLTN vehicle, to use as reference when needed. Finally, make sure to take all parts and hard case associated with each GPS unit when visiting a park and do not mix parts between units. Even though parts can look alike, at times they have different voltages that will cause harm when used with the wrong GPS unit.

IV.   Glossary

Features: Refers to what item is being collected – point, line or polygon.

GPS: Global Positioning System

Multipath: GPS signals that have been reflected off of objects before being received by a GPS unit, instead of a direct signal. Multipath increases GPS error.

PDOP: Position Dilution of Precision. It is an indication of the accuracy of the calculated position based on the location of the satellites in the constellation. If satellite positions do not allow the use of coordinate geometry, then accurate ground locations can not be triangulated from them.

Positions: The number of signals received from the GPS satellites that are used to make a feature.

Post-processed Differential Correction: A method that reduces GPS measurement error by using base station data to correct the GPS rover file once field collection is done. (More accurate than real-time correction)

Real-time Correction: A method that reduces GPS measurement error by using WAAS (Wide Area Augmentation System) to correct the GPS on the fly.

Rover File: GPS file collected in the field.

UTM: Universal Transverse Mercator

Standard Operating Procedure 4: Establishing and Marking Permanent Sample Sites

Version 1.01 (June 2009)

Revision History Log:

Previous Version #	Revision Date	Author	Changes Made	Reason for Change	New Version #
1.00 6/18/2009		K.M. James	Minor updates	Reflect current methods	1.01

This SOP gives step-by-step instructions for establishing and marking permanent sites. It provides instructions for permanently marking transect ends and the correct procedure for labeling rebar tags. It also explains the procedure for collecting the relevant data and filling in Data Form 1 "Site Establishment Sheet for Plant Community Monitoring" located in SOP #1.

I.   Equipment List

- GPS unit (1)
- Clinometer (1)
- Compass (2)
- Digital Camera
- Flagging – for marking rebar and witness trees
- Leatherman or pliers
- Maps
- Photobook
- Rebar (4)
- Hammer – for hammering rebar
- Tags and wire
- Tapes (4)
- Yellow Caps – fit over the ends of each rebar to increase rebar visibility

II.   Procedures

1.   Sites are located within each park in a systematic random manner. A grid overlay is first created for a park using a random bearing. The vertices of the grid are spatially referenced to form a matrix of potential sample points. Soil, aspect and management unit

attributes are assigned to each matrix point using a GIS to identify a pool of points for each stratum.

2. In the field, points are visited in random order. When arriving at a point, the suitability of the area as a site is assessed. If the site is suitable, a permanent site is installed. Alternatively, the reason for rejection is noted and the next point visited until all sites are located. Often the initial reference frame is modified after the first field visit to exclude areas that are not suitable for sampling, such as areas that are particularly narrow, steep, or erosive.

3. The paired transects are 50 m long, 20 m apart and run parallel to each other and to the elevation contours. Once the decision is made to locate a site in a particular location, the upslope transect is laid out and surveyed. First, a rebar is established at the first corner and an azimuth is determined that runs parallel to the contours. This corner is typically the beginning of the A line, unless topography does not allow it. A tape is then run out 50 m to the end point of the transect and another rebar is driven in the ground. At an azimuth perpendicular to the first transect line, a distance is measured 20 m to the end point of the second transect. This is typically the end of the down-slope transect or transect B. Once a rebar is established for the end point of the B line a back azimuth is shot to parallel the A line and a distance of 50 m is run and the final corner of the site is established.

4. Once all four rebar are established, they are tagged with brass tags stamped with the site number and rebar designation. For example, 10 AS is site number 10 and it is the start (S) of the A line (the upslope transect). The tags are wired to the rebar using pliers or a leatherman. A plastic yellow cap is also placed on the end of the rebar for increased visibility and to protect tractor tires/cow hoofs from damage. A digital photograph is taken at each rebar looking down the transect. If available, two trees per rebar are monumented as witness trees. Information is collected for each tree including species, diameter at breast height (dbh), azimuth from tree to rebar and distance to rebar. An aluminum tag with duplicate information to the rebar tag is nailed to the tree using aluminum nails at eye height pointing towards the rebar.

5. Once the rebar are permanent, relocation data for each transect is collected. GPS coordinates for the rebar ends of each transect are taken using the procedure described in SOP #3 "Using GPS". Metadata are then recorded, including type of monumenting and azimuth (see section III for detailed instructions on Data Form 1). Ancillary evidence of disturbance such as old roadbeds, fences and animal burrows is also noted when sample units are established.

III. Collecting and Recording Data

When a site is initially established, Data Form 1 "Site Establishment Sheet for Plant Community Monitoring" is filled out by the field crew involved in the site installation. The intent of the survey is to prompt the field crew to assist in characterizing the structure and composition of the site. Several of the questions are consistent with the National Vegetation Classification Standards (NVCS) and data from these sections will help us to fit survey areas into that classification system. Although several of the questions are somewhat subjective, the information provide can be of tremendous value when consistency and good judgment are practiced in the field. SOP #1 provides an example of the site establishment data sheet. Often the establishment sheet is tailored to a specific park, especially such fields as vegetation type. Below are instructions for filling out a sample datasheet from TAPR. Notes about the sites should also be noted on this datasheet, including information about disturbance regimes.

Park: A unique 4 digit code (example: TAPR Tallgrass Prairie National Preserve)

Site number: A unique sample unit identification number (example: TAPR_VegMon_7)

Pasture/Unit: Management unit or pasture name (example: Crusher Pasture)

Establishment date: Include month / day / year (mm/dd/yyyy)

Established by: Provide the unique initials of the people present when the sample unit was established. (example: ANS, Alicia N. Sasseen)

Soil series / site selection information: Provide if known

Azimuth of transects (from 0 – 50 m): Recorded to the nearest one degree

Monumenting: Describe what forms of permanent marking were utilized – GPS and/or witness trees

Monumenting notes: Expand on the form of permanent marking used.

Slope angle (%): Enter the steepness of the slope surface. Sight slope angle at both transect <u>Start</u> and <u>Finish</u>, with slope reader standing on A line and second person standing on B line. The sighting poles should be used for a more accurate reading. If a second person is not available, take readings in a kneeling position to improve accuracy, sighting to the same height above the ground as your eye when taking each reading. Record each reading in percent (**not degrees**), which is usually the right-hand column of numbers in the clinometer. It is important to remember that percent slope changes more quickly than degrees slope, e.g., 45 degrees slope = 100 percent slope.

Slope aspect (deg): Dominant aspect reading are taken at three points in the plot, at the beginning (<u>Start</u>), middle (<u>Center</u>) and end (<u>Finish</u>) of transect A. Slope aspect can be obtained by determining the main direction that water would flow from the observed point. Slope aspect is measured to the nearest degree.

Terrain shape: Using the clinometer and standing at plot center, slope inclination readings are recorded at 90 degree intervals starting with the dominant aspect of the plot and moving clockwise around the plot. All angles should be sighted to a distance of 15 m from the plot center. If a second person is unavailable, take readings in a kneeling position to improve accuracy. All angles are recorded in percent (not degrees) with attention to whether the angle is below level (downhill) or above level (uphill) relative to the plot center. All readings are given a plus sign or a minus sign to denote uphill and downhill angles from plot center, respectively. It is important to accurately define the 90 degree intervals and take measurements carefully.

Topographic position: Define the overall topographic position of the site using the provided NVCS terminology and definitions. Categories include:

Level – no slope

Lower-slope – gently inclined surface at the base of a slope, commonly gentle and almost linear in surface profile

Mid-slope – intermediate slope position

Upper-slope (high slope, shoulder slope) – the uppermost inclined surface at the top of a slope, typically convex in profile

Crest (interfluve, summit, ridge) – linear top of a ridge, hill or mountain; the elevated area between two drainage-ways that sheds water

Ledge (terrace) – nearly level shelf interrupting a steep slope or cliff face

Depression – bottom surface of a basin

Streambed – bed of single or braided watercourse, typically barren and formed of modern alluvium

Hydrologic regime: Define the overall hydrology of the site using the provided descriptive modifiers from NVCS. Categories include:

Permanently flooded – water covers the surface at all times of the year in all years

Semi-permanently flooded – surface water persists throughout the growing season in most years; land surface is generally saturated when the water level drops below the surface

Seasonally/temporarily flooded – surface water is present for extended periods during the growing season, but is absent by the end of the growing season in most years; the water table is normally very variable

Intermittently flooded – surface water is present during times of increased precipitation, but generally dry

Seep – intermittent, seasonal, or permanent flow of water from a subterranean source that is generally confined to a relatively discrete area

Upland – the site cannot be characterized as a wetland as it either sheds or absorbs water quickly; the water table is almost always well below the soil surface

Surface water: This is the distance to standing water, categories to choose from are: (1) in plot; (2) <50 m away; and (3) >50 m away.

Vegetation type: Circle corresponding description, sample categories include:
Upland Prairie – prairie with well-drained soils

Riparian Woodland – open stands of trees with crowns not usually touching, generally forming 25-60% cover, located in riparian area

Rocky site – prairie area with large amount of exposed rock

Vegetation Community Monitoring Protocol
For the Heartland Inventory and Monitoring Network

Standard Operating Procedure 5: Measuring Frequency and Cover of Herbaceous and Shrub Species

Version 1.0 (December 2004)

Revision History Log:

Previous Version #	Revision Date	Author	Changes Made	Reason for Change	New Version #

This SOP gives step-by-step instructions for obtaining frequency and cover estimates of herbaceous and shrub species in the nested circular plots. Detailed instructions are provided for locating the 10 m^2 along the paired transects, as well as locating the nested 0.01 m^2, 0.1 m^2 and 1.0 m^2 plots. This SOP also describes the procedure for filling in Data Form 2 "Herbaceous Data Collection Form" and Data Form 3 "Unknown Data Sheet". Examples of these data forms are available in SOP #1.

I.   Equipment List

- Clip boards (2)
- Herbaceous species data sheets (2 sets)
- Flagging tape (to make hoops and other equipment easily visible)
- Flags (to mark questionable plants)
- Pencils, extra pencil lead and erasers
- Plots (10 m^2, 0.01 m^2, 0.1 m^2 and 1 m^2, two sets)
- Plant press
- Plant species list for site
- Rebar (to replace missing rebar)
- Rope and stakes (for use in wooded areas as 10 m^2 plot)
- 50 meter tapes (2)
- Unknown specimen book
- Unknown data forms
- Vegetation identification keys as needed
- Write-In-Rain blank data sheets (to avoid confusion with regular paper, keep labeled)

II.   Procedures

Site and Plot Setup
Laying out Transects: Each monitoring site includes two 50 meter transects (A and B) spaced 20

m apart (Figure 5.1). The ends of both transects are marked with rebar stakes and metal tags indicating the start and finish. The metal tag on the stake located at the "start" of both transects is marked with the following information: site identification (the number "1, 2, 3….."), transect identification ("A" or "B") and the letter "S". The metal tag on the stake located at the "finish" of both transects is marked with site identification (the number "1, 2, 3….."), transect identification ("A" or "B") and the letter "F". It is absolutely crucial to begin at the start and to know which transect line you are sampling. These two factors relate directly to the location of each plot along the length of the transect.

Once both ends of a transect have been located using GPS, one person each stands at the located rebar stakes and a third person lays down the 50 m tape. The line is stretched as taut as possible to avoid curvature in the line. Curvature in the line would result in variation in the location of each plot along the line. Under windy conditions this can be a difficult endeavor. All members of the sampling team assist in locating rebar stakes and setting up transect lines.

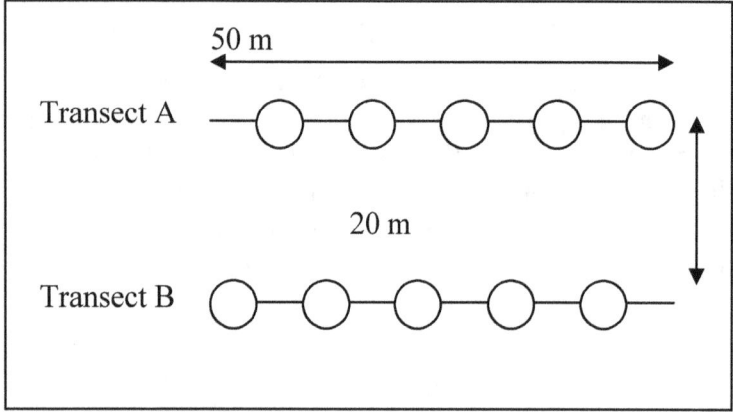

Figure 5.1. HTLN site showing 50 m long paired transects with 10 systematically arranged plots, 10 m² in size, for sampling ground flora.

Sampling teams: One sampling team, each consisting of a scribe and a botanist, is assigned to a transect line. The sampling team is responsible for the following: (1) assembling their sampling frame; (2) collecting all of the required data, including metadata for the transect and plot data; (3) collecting and describing any unknown plants encountered and relaying the information to the project botanist before leaving the site; and (4) ensuring that all equipment, including sampling frames, meter tape, flags, flagging, data sheets and clip boards, make it to the next site.

Laying out the nested plots and 10 m² plots: Herbaceous and shrub species frequency and cover data are collected in five 10 m² circular plots located along each transect, spaced 10 m apart (Figure 5.1). Along transect A, plots are centered at 10 m, 20 m, 30 m, 40 m and 50 m. Along transect B, plots are centered at 0 m, 10 m, 20 m, 30 m and 40 m. Beginning at the "start" of the transect, the 10 m² plot, fully assembled, is centered on the first sampling location. The sampling frame is centered by laying the center of the cross-bars that divides the plot into four quarters directly on the taut tape over the desired meter mark. Align one length of the cross-bars with the tape stretched between the rebar stakes. At this point, the large outer plot is ready for sampling.

44

Within the 10 m^2 plot are placed three nested circular plots, called nested frequency plots (Figure 5.2). Nested frequency data is collected using small circular plots, one positioned inside the other and noting the species rooted within. The small plots intentionally favor capturing mostly dominant species so that even small shifts in their abundance may be observed. The sampling of the nested frequency plots occurs in conjunction with sampling for frequency and cover. The circular subplots used in this study are 0.01 m^2, 0.1 m^2 and 1 m^2. The nested plots are laid on the edge of the 10 m^2 sampling frame, towards the "start" of the transect line where the frame crosses the meter tape. It is important to be diligent about the placement of the plots to ensure consistent sampling from year to year.

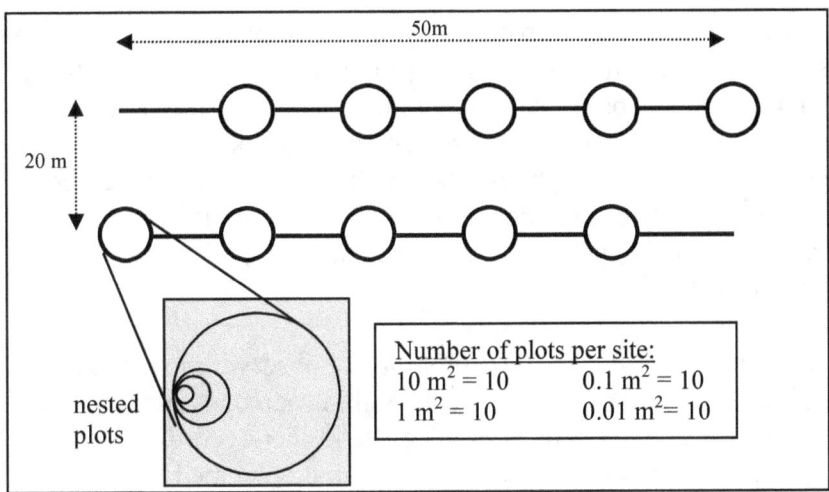

Figure 5.2. Site with nested frequency plots.

In summary:

1. Pull the transect line as taunt as possible between the two rebar at the ends.

2. Consult plot records and transect tags to ensure that the "A" and "B" transect lines (recorded on the tags which are attached to the rebar as "A" and "B") are not reversed.

3. Always start the tape at the beginning of the transect (recorded on the tags around the rebar as "S" for "start").

4. Place the center of each 10 m^2 plot on the meter marker, where the support bars cross.

5. Along transect A, space the 10 m^2 plots every 10 m beginning at 10 m, so that the 10 m^2 plots are centered on the 10 m, 20 m, 30 m, 40 m and 50 m marks.

6. Along transect B, space the 10 m^2 plots every 10 m beginning at 0 m, so that the 10 m^2 plots are centered on the 0 m, 10 m, 20 m, 30 m and 40 m marks.

7. Nest the circular 0.01 m^2, 0.1 m^2 and 1.0 m^2 plots where the "edge" of the 10 m^2 plot crosses the tape nearest to the "S" end of the transect.

III. Collecting and Recording Data

Collecting Species Data

With the nested subplots located inside the larger sampling frame, it is time to begin collecting data. Before collecting data for any plot, double check that the plot's location corresponds with the plot number on the data sheet. For each plot there is a data sheet labeled with the plot number and the names of the species found in the plot during previous sample efforts (see Data Form 2 in Apendix 1.1 of SOP #1). This plot data is not shared with the observer until he/she has completed their search of all plots for plants.

Data collection begins in the smallest plot first. The observer identifies to species (if possible) all herbaceous plants and woody shrubs rooted within the 0.01 m^2 plot. If a plant is rooted entirely underneath the plot frame, it is not counted as being within that plot. Generally, the plots sit on or close to the ground when sampling. However, tall or dense vegetation, rocks, or an otherwise uneven surface may prevent this. In such cases, simply estimate as fairly as you can whether a borderline species appears to be rooted inside or outside the plot. All species with live plant material rooted within the plot are recorded on the data form and a check is made in the 0.01 m^2 column next to each species as it is found.

Once all plant species have been identified within the 0.01 m^2 plot, the observer moves to the next plot (0.1 m^2 plot) and so on until the 10 m^2 plot is reached. Within each consecutively greater sized plot, all new plants encountered are called and recorded. When recording species for plots, a species should always be recorded in the first plot in which it is located.

The search for plants in the 10 m^2 plot is facilitated by the cross-bars separating the plot into four quarters. The observer must take care not to trample the plot. This is integral to the success of any long-term monitoring projects. Once the observer has completed his/her search of the 10 m^2 plot, the species list is consulted to look for possible mistakes in species identifications and missed species. This list provides the names, but not associated cover values, of species previously collected in a plot for comparison to those currently collected. If a species was previously collected but is now missing, the plot is double checked to ensure the species has not been overlooked. The species may be absent but may surface in a later sampling period, or its record in previous years may reflect a change in species identification or sampling error. At this point, any lingering questions on species identification should be communicated to the project botanist or leader. He/she will decide if it is necessary to fill out an "unknown" record and give the species of question an unknown number and name. See the section below entitled "Unknown Specimens" for more details.

Estimates of Foliar Cover

For each species present, a visual estimate of foliar cover is made within the 10 m^2 sampling plot. The estimate is a vertical projection of foliar cover onto the ground surface. The foliar cover of each species is estimated using a cover class index modified from Daubenmire (1959, Table 5.1). Only species rooted in the plot are recorded and included in estimates of foliar cover. Each individual percentage value alone cannot exceed 100%, but when combined the cover value for a plot may be greater than 100%.

Table 5.1. Modified Daubenmire cover value scale used to determine herbaceous/shrub species cover for the HTLN Parks.

Cover Class Codes	Range of Cover (%)	Class Midpoints (%)
7 95-100		97.5
6 75-95		85.0
5 50-75		62.5
4 25-50		37.5
3 5-25		15.0
2 1-5		2.5
1 0-0.99		0.5

Recording Data

For each plot, there is a corresponding "Herbaceous Data Collection Form" (see SOP #1 Data Form 2 for an example for fall herbaceous collection at EFMO). When first arriving at a site, each sampling team is handed a set of data sheets that corresponds to the plots along the transect to which they are assigned. When starting each new plot, it is important to make sure data is being transcribed to the correct data sheet. Record the following information on each data sheet:

Date: Include month (mm) / day (dd) / year (yy).

Collector's initials: The unique initials of the first and last name of each person in the field crew collecting data. If initials of two or more persons are the same, include a middle initial or some other distinguishing initial.

Start Time: Time when field crew begins collecting plot data at the monitoring site.

End time: Time when field crew finished collecting plot data at the monitoring site.

Data entered (ini): Date when data is entered into the computer. Include month (mm) / day (dd) / year (yy) and the initials of the person conducting the data entry.

Verified (ini): Date when data is verified by comparing the paper data to the printout of the data in the database. Include month (mm) / day (dd) / year (yy) and the initials of the person conducting the verification.

Data Form for the Sample Period

A plot datasheet with a list of species previously encountered in the plot is provided in a column on the right-hand side of the datasheet for reference. Species found in this sampling period are written on the left-hand side in the column provided using eight letter acronyms (first four letters of genus and first four letters of species). An "X" is then made in the box corresponding to the plot in which the first specimen of each particular species was found. For all species, cover is estimated within the 10 m^2 plot. Cover class codes are recorded in the column titled "Cover". After sampling, the species list providing the names of all species once present in the plot is used to determine if any less common species were missed. Estimates of ground cover are collected for the categories listed: bare soil, bare rock, grass litter, leaf litter, woody debris and unvegetated are recorded in the column titled "Cover" using the same modified Daubenmire cover class codes (Table 5.1). SOP #7 "Measuring Ground Cover" contains more detailed information on collecting ground cover.

Unknown Specimens

Sometimes species determinations of individual plants encountered in sampling are difficult or uncertain. When this situation occurs, the area surrounding the plot should be searched, looking particularly for a specimen of the unknown that is in flower or fruit, or perhaps is a specimen from last year with its flowering stalk still intact. These may assist in correctly identifying the species in the plot. Most of these plants are not entirely "unknown" species. Rather, they are of a species that is known but sometimes difficult to distinguish from another given the timing of sampling. For example, small *Bouteloua curtipendula* plants may be confused with *Bouteloua hirsuta*. Both of these species are common and often confidently identified during our various sampling procedures. If the evidence does not favor one species over another, then the next broader taxonomic grouping can be recorded. In the above example, "*Bouteloua* spp." could be recorded. This name would be sufficient until species-level identification is available (e.g., during a subsequent sampling the plant is found in the same location in flower, seed, or fruit, aiding correct identification).

Plants not immediately identified in the plot are recorded on the data sheet with an unknown specimen code (<park code> <unknown number> <date>, e.g., WICRunk2_7_03). A sample of that species is then collected. Because of the long-term nature of the monitoring, collecting outside the plot is preferred. If a specimen does not occur outside the plot, a portion of the plant from inside the plot can be collected, but at no time should the roots be dug up or the entire plant be collected from inside the plot. Collecting the roots and/or the entire above-ground portion of the plant may affect future sampling events.

For each unknown specimen, there is a corresponding Unknown Record sheet (see SOP#1 Data Form 3). The more detailed a definition of each characteristic, the greater the possibility of a future identification. Use the following procedure when filling out the Unknown Record sheet:

Park: A four letter alpha code unique to a particular park (example: WICR – Wilson's Creek National Battlefield, Missouri)

Transect and Plot: Vegetation monitoring site, transect and plot number (example: VegMon 5 _20B – monitoring site 5, transect B, plot 20)

Date: Include month (mm) / day (dd) / year (yy)

Unknown Code: A unique code using <park code> <unknown number> <date>, e.g., WICRunk2_7_03

Plant type and General Description: Circle the appropriate category and provide a detailed description of the overall appearance

Most Salient Feature: The feature that identifies this plant from all others; a unique characteristic

Leaf Characteristics: Describe the leaf type, leaf margin, leaf surface, petiole, etc.

Stem Characteristics: Describe the shape, pubescence, markings and color of the stem, as well as the bud characteristics.

Flower Characteristics: Describe the floral formula, location (axillary or terminal), habit (indeterminate or determinate), pubescence and color.

General and Microhabitat Characteristics: List other species located in the general vicinity, selecting the more conservative species in the area. Describe the microhabitat in which it was found.

Collected: Circle yes or no, whether a specimen was collected.

Best Guess: Preliminary guess about species in field.

Confirmed to be: After consultation of reference books and/or herbarium, the species determined.

Vegetation Community Monitoring Protocol
For the Heartland Inventory and Monitoring Network

Standard Operating Procedure 7: Measuring Ground Cover

Version 1.00 (December 2004)

Revision History Log:

Previous Version #	Revision Date	Author	Changes Made	Reason for Change	New Version #

This SOP gives step-by-step instructions for measuring ground cover in the circular 10 m^2 plots (1.78 m in diameter). It also explains the procedure for filling in the ground cover section of the Data Form 2 "Herbaceous Data Collection Form" located in SOP #1. Refer to SOP #5 for details concerning the establishment of the sample unit and the 10 m^2 plots, as well as details on the plant species data collected concurrently with the ground cover data.

I.   Equipment List - No additional equipment is needed to collect ground cover data concurrently with species plot data.

II.   Collecting and Recording Data

Ground cover attributes of each sample unit are measured to describe physical changes resulting from management activities. The ground-level cover of bare soil, bare rock, tree leaf litter, grass litter and woody debris is estimated for each 10 m^2 plot. This will allow for exploration of correlative relationships between compositional changes and environmental attributes.
In each 10 m^2 plot, the percent cover of bare soil, bare rock, grass litter, leaf litter, woody debris and total percent unvegetated is estimated using the same modified-Daubenmire cover classes used for plant species foliar cover estimates (Table 7.1). Ground cover information is recorded in the lower left hand corner of the data sheet used for plant species data (Data Form 2 "Herbaceous Data Collection Form"). Estimates of ground cover are taken before species plot data are recorded to minimize the trampling effect on ocular estimates. As with plant species cover, the sum of the individual ground cover categories can be greater than the value recorded for the total category "Unvegetated".

Table 7.1. Modified-Daubenmire cover value scale used to determine unvegetated substrate cover for the HTLN Parks.

Cover Class Codes	Range of Cover (%)	Class Midpoints (%)
7 95-100		97.5
6 75-95		85.0
5 50-75		62.5
4 25-50		37.5
3 5-25		15.0
2 1-5		2.5
1 0-0.99		0.5

III.   Ground Cover Definitions

Several ground cover categories exist for unvegetated substrates. These categories, modified from EPA's EMAP-SW Streams Field Operations Manual, are defined as follows:

Bare Soil – exposed soil including clay, silt, fine sand and well-disintegrated dark duff and humus (see "grass litter" below).

Rock – loose or fixed rocks ranging in size from a coarse grain of sand (approximately 2 mm or less) to larger than a small car (>4000 mm).

Grass Litter – dead grass leaf and stem litter no longer standing – should be distinguishable as grass or light in color. There is no concise point at which disintegrated grass litter is considered duff or humus and thereby included in the 'bare soil' category. In making cover estimates for a 10 m^2 plot, lightly colored detritus is generally considered grass litter and darker areas as soil. A guideline consistent with this practice is to consider light-colored particles that are otherwise indistinguishable as grass litter and dark colored particles as soil.

Leaf litter – leaf litter from deciduous tree and woody shrub species (examples of woody shrub species include *Ceanothus* spp., *Cornus drummondii*, *Rhus glabra and Symphoricarpos orbiculatus*).

Woody debris – all woody debris regardless of size

Unvegetated – this is the area in the plot not occupied by the stems of the growing plants. It includes all the previous categories. This often has a large cover value since the stems of herbaceous plants do not comprise significant basal area.

Standard Operating Procedure 8: Conducting the Woody Species Sampling

Version 1.0 (December 2004)

Revision History Log:

Prev. Version #	Revision Date	Author	Changes Made	Reason for Change	New Version #
1.0 07/09		KM James	Additional data collection	Add ability to track changes in stand structure	2.0

This SOP gives step-by-step instructions for sampling the woody species located in the overstory, understory and seedling/sapling layers of the vegetation macroplot. Woody species data are collected in conjunction with the herbaceous sampling schedule, since they utilize the same macroplot (Figure 8.1). This SOP describes the procedure for collecting data and filling in Data Form 4 "Woody Species Overstory and Understory Data Collection Form" and the seedling/sapling and densiometer portions of the Data Form 2 "Herbaceous Data Collection Form" (see SOP #1 for Data Forms).

I.   Procedures

Once distance tapes are stretched from start to finish of both transects, enter the following standard information on the top of Data Form 4 "Woody Species Overstory and Understory Data Collection Form" (see SOP #1):

Transect #: This is the sample unit number located on the rebar tags at the beginning and end of each transect.

Date (mm/dd/yyyy): Write in the month (2 digits), day (2 digits) and year (4 digits) in the form shown. Include the forward slash. Examples are 05/02/2004 and 06/30/2004.

Collectors: Fill in the three initials of the people conducting the woody species surveys using capital letters. If you do not have a middle name, put an underscore for your middle initial. In the database, these initials will correspond to the full name and contact information for that person. (The 3-character initials in the database must be unique and if two people have the same initials, one should be given an honorary middle name.)

Overstory and Understory Measurement
1.   Measure all tree species (Figure 8.1), both alive and standing or leaning dead, ≥ 5cm in dbh (diameter at breast height), in the 20 m x 50 m area (0.1 ha) located between transects A and

B (Figure 8.1). Working from the Start end of the transects, move through the plot systematically taking care not to miss trees. Each tree is marked using a chalk paddle as it is measured. This is done to ensure each overstory tree is sampled only once. For parks with densely wooded areas, future provisions may reduce the area sampled for tree species with DBH ≥5cm but <15cm to a 10 m x 20 m area. The 10 m x 20 m subplot will be centered in the existing plot where tree species ≥15cm in DBH are measured (Figure 8.2).

2. Each tree is identified to species, if possible. Tree species are recorded using a species code consisting of the first four letters of both the genus and the species epithet. For example, *Quercus velutina* is recorded as QUERVELU. Diameter at breast height is measured 1.372 m (4.5 feet) from root collar of all tree species ≥5cm in dbh, both alive and standing or leaning dead. In sloping areas, dbh is measured with an observer standing on the uphill side of tree. Diameter at breast height is measured to the nearest tenth of a centimeter. If a distortion of the bole occurs at 1.372m, dbh is measured just above the distortion. Species with split trunks below 1.372 m (coppice trees) are measured as individual trees with each stem receiving dbh measurements. Coppice trees with split trunks above 1.372 m are measured as one tree and given a single dbh. All overstory trees are recorded on the data form 4 "Woody Species Overstory and Understory Data Collection Form".

3. A condition code is assigned to each tree using the following codes:
   a. L = Live
   b. D = Standing Dead/Snag

4. Each live tree in the overstory is assigned a crown position code (Table 8.2). Canopy position of the live overstory trees is assessed using crown position (Avery and Burkhart 1963). Figure 8.3 illustrates relative canopy position for each crown position code (Fire Monitoring Handbook 2003).

Trees are considered alive if they have any living parts (leaves, buds, cambium) at or above the point of diameter measurement. Trees that have been temporarily defoliated are still alive. A designation of coppice form (Yes or No) is also recorded.

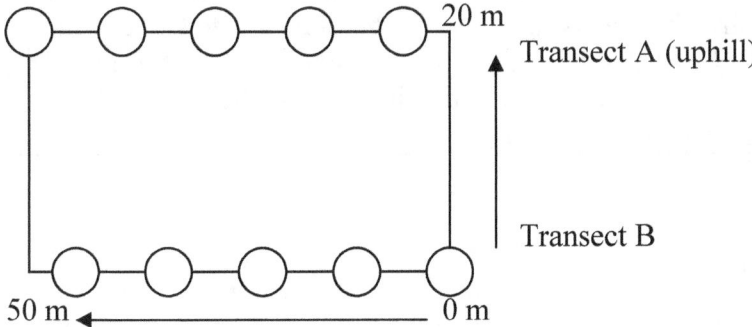

Figure 8.1. Diagram displaying paired transects creating the 20 m x 50 m macroplot for tree species sampling with the smaller 10 m^2 herbaceous vegetation sampling subplots. The 10 m^2 subplots are also where seedlings and saplings <5cm dbh are tallied.

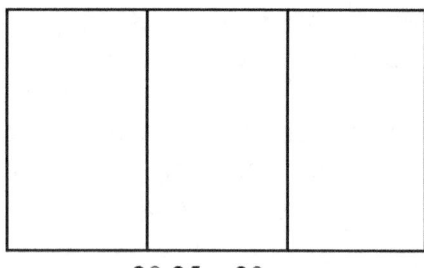

30 25m 20

Figure 8.2. Diagram displaying paired transects creating the 20 m x 50 m macroplot for tree species sampling with the provisional 10 m x 20 m subset plot for measuring understory tree species ≥5cm and <15cm.

Table 8.2. Descriptions of live tree crown position codes (Fire Monitoring Handbook 2003).

Code	Position	Description
1	Dominant	Trees with crowns extending above the general level of the crown cover and receiving full light from above and at least partly from the side; these trees are larger than the average trees in the stand and have well-developed crowns, but may be somewhat crowded on the sides.
2	Co-dominant	Trees with crowns forming the general level of the crown cover and receiving full light from above, but comparatively little from the sides; these trees usually have medium-size crowns and are more or less crowded on the sides.
3	Intermediate	Trees shorter than those in the two preceding classes, but with crowns either below or extending into the crown cover formed by co-dominant and dominant trees, receiving little direct light from above and none from the sides; these trees usually have small crowns and are considerably crowded on the sides.
4	Subcanopy	Trees with crowns below the general level of the crown cover and receiving no direct light from above or from the sides.
5 Open	Growth /Isolated	Trees receiving full sunlight from above and all sides. Typically, these are single trees of the same general height and size as other trees in the area, but where the stand is open and trees are widely separated so dominance is difficult to determine.

Figure 8.3. Illustrated canopy position of crown position codes (Fire Monitoring Handbook 2003).

Seedling & Sapling Measurement

For tree species <5cm DBH (termed the seedling/sapling layer), sampling occurs in the ten 10 m^2 herbaceous plots during the herbaceous sampling using Field Form 2 "Herbaceous Data Collection Form" located in SOP #1. For each 10 m^2 herbaceous plot, the number of stems for each tree species are tallied in three size classes:

    a. Seedlings <0.5m in height

    b. Small saplings ≥0.5m in height and <2.54cm DBH

    c. Large saplings ≥2.54cm DBH to <5.0cm DBH

If unsure of identification of small oak species, lump into white oak group or red oak group. These data are recorded on the herbaceous data sheets located in SOP #1. Estimates of foliar cover are not measured.

Canopy Measurement

Densiometers are used at each 10 m^2 plot (Figure 8.1) to observe amount of canopy cover. The spherical densiometer consists of a concave mirror with 24, ¼ inch squares engraved on the surface. Standing over the plot center, four densiometer readings are taken facing the four cardinal directions (N, E, S, W). The densiometer is held level 12" to 18" in front of body at breast height, so the operator's head is outside of the grid area. The 24 squares on the densiometer are divided into 96 dots, assuming equally spaced dots in each square of the grid. Readings are taken of the number of dots out of 96 that are covered by canopy (green leaves). If canopy openings are counted rather than canopy closure, subtract from 96 to obtain canopy coverage. Densiometer readings are recorded on the top of the herbaceous vegetation sampling data sheet. The number of dots covered by canopy will be converted to percent canopy coverage (multiplied by 1.04) during the data summary process.

Standard Operating Procedure 11: Data Management

Version 2.00 (May 2009)

Revision History Log:

Prev. Version #	Revision Date	Author	Changes Made	Reason for Change	New Version #
1.00 5/27/09		G.A. Rowell	Revised entire SOP	Reflect updated VEGMON database	2.00

This SOP describes procedures for managing the Heartland Inventory and Monitoring Network (HTLN) database for plant communities. The plant community database is called 'VEGMON'. The database is developed in Microsoft Access. This document addresses procedures for data entry, verification, validation, export, security and availability. Parks are referenced throughout the database using the standard National Park Service four-letter abbreviations. Database users should become familiar with the park abbreviations. Park names, abbreviations and links to internet URLs are available through the opening form (the "Switchboard") of the database.

I. Data Model

VEGMON has a hierarchical design based on the NPS NRDT standard. Like most monitoring databases, VEGMON is event-driven. Locations and sampling periods should be maintained at the top of the hierarchy (they are related one-to-many with other tables in the database). Locations in the database represent permanent transects within parks. Sampling periods represent a field trip lasting several days. The sampling period ID is the start date for the sampling period. VEGMON contains 18 data tables (including look-up, enumeration and reference tables). Core event tables contain field data. Examples of core event tables are tbl_VegMonData and tbl_GroundCoverData among others. Core event tables are supported by several look-up tables such as tbl_Species_LU, tbl_CoverClasses_LU and tbl_GroundCover_LU. An entity relationship diagram (ERD) of the basic design is given in Figure 11.1.

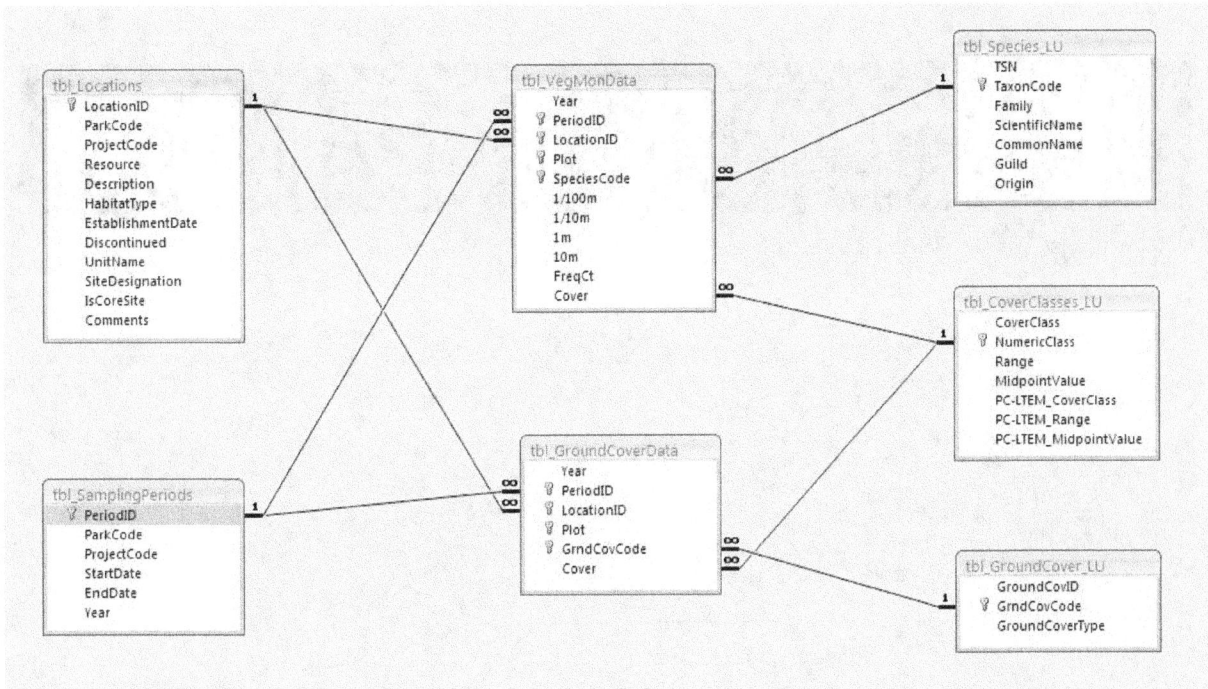

Figure 11.1. ERD for VEGMON 7.1. Database events include understory forest and prairie observations.

II.   Data Preparation

Quality assurance and quality control procedures are important components in any monitoring project. Sampling data (i.e., transect location, plot size, percent canopy and species abundance data) should be recorded and checked for completeness either before leaving a site or within 24 hours of data recording. This will aid in verification and validation of the data after entry into the database. To prevent the complete loss of field form data due to unforeseen circumstances (i.e., fire or flood in the workplace), all field sheets should be photocopied and a hard copy stored in a location separate from the original. Field sheets should be scanned into a computer and electronic copies of the data sheets stored on the HTLN server located at Wilson's Creek National Battlefield, Republic, Missouri. This will ensure that at least one copy of the field sheets is available for data entry and verification.

III.   Data Entry

Data entry is accomplished using several forms. The user interface begins with the switchboard. The switchboard reflects the overall design of the database.

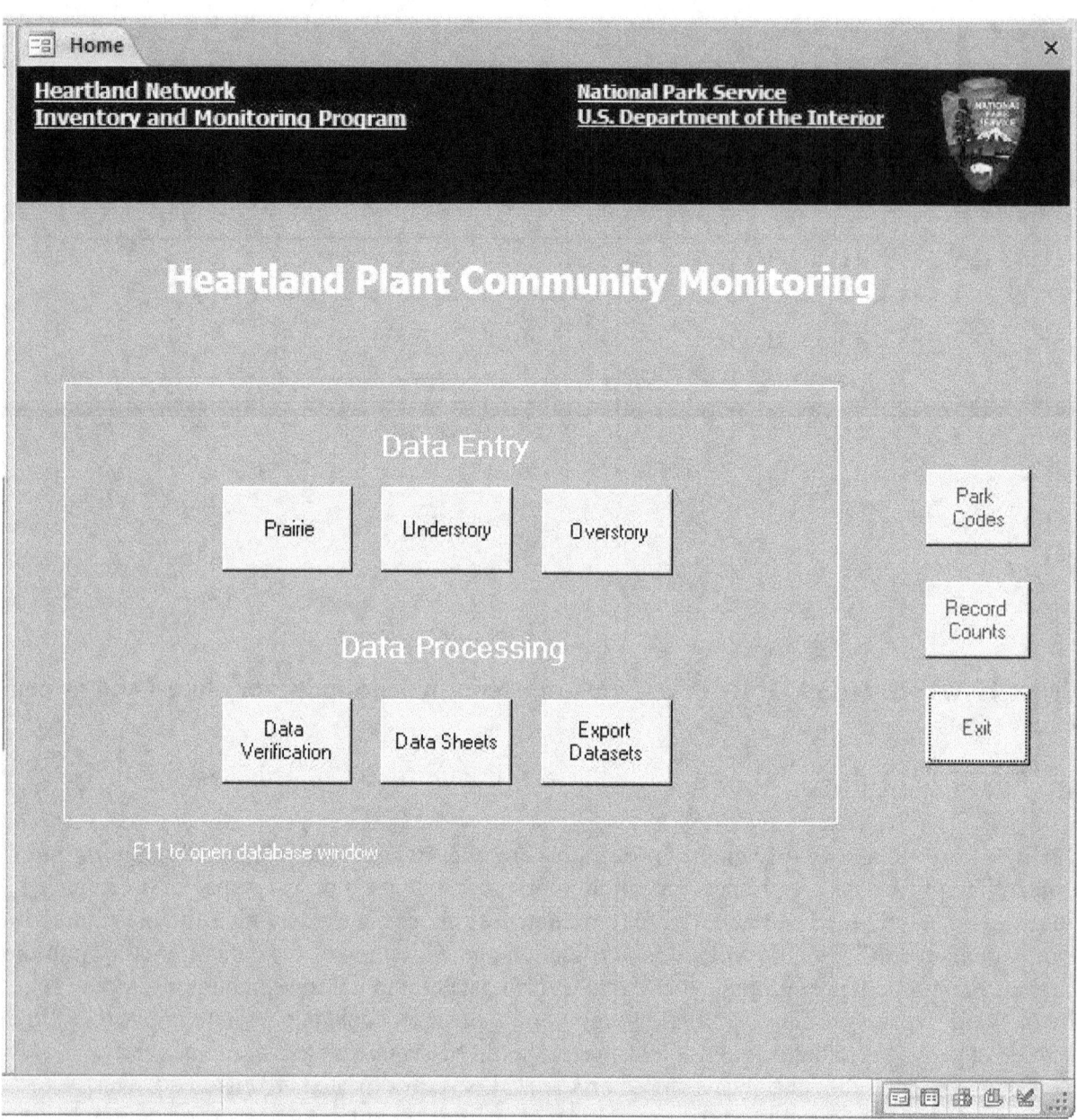

Figure 11.2. VEGMON database switchboard.

Data entry procedures are divided into three categories based on their plant community data type: Prairie, Understory and Overstory. Field procedures for gathering these different datasets are described in SOPs #5, #7 and #8. To ensure that each observation is associated with a location and sampling period, new reference locations and new sampling periods must be added prior to data entry. New locations must be added to the database when new sampling sites are established at a park. New sampling periods will be required with each additional field season.

IV.   Data Verification

Data verification immediately follows data entry. Computer records should be verified for accuracy by comparing each computer record against field datasheets. Hard copy of data records should be used in the verification against field data to minimize error. Compare the output directly with original field data sheets to identify missing, mismatched, or redundant records. The verification step should be completed by staff other than those doing data entry if at all possible. Following verification, the project manager should recheck 10% of the records. The verification and recheck steps should be repeated until no errors are discovered.

V.   Data Validation

Validation procedures introduce additional requirements on data entry. Nominal data should be restricted to predefined classes as maintained in look-up tables. Event table – look-up table relationships should be maintained with referential constraints. In other words, the look-up table primary key must be unique and event table foreign keys must reference values from the domain of look-up table primary keys. These features should be built into the database. They are used throughout VEGMON. SQL queries should be used for further data validation. Frequency distributions should be calculated for nominal classes using a DISTINCT query and COUNT. Unexpected class frequencies may indicate problems.

Continuous data should be examined closely for irregularities. Sample sizes and range in values should be examined in all instances. Missing values, zeros and negative values may indicate data problems. Histograms and descriptive statistics such as mean, standard deviation, median and mode may also be helpful. Check for missing locations using a DISTINCT query. Check for differences in locations between years using OUTER JOINs.

VI.   Exporting Data

VEGMON features a set of export queries that facilitate data transfer into software packages such as spreadsheets and statistical packages. Each export category follows the basic organization of plant communities as indicated by the user interface above.

Export data sets are organized by park and year. This organization should help the project investigator to make comparison of the same parameters between years. This organization may aid the researcher in identifying trends in those measurables that are high priority in a given park.

The project investigator should seriously consider exporting data into statistical packages that will allow further assessment of the data in terms of quality control. For example, the researcher must decide whether an outlier constitutes a natural member of the data distribution or is, in fact, a result of user error during the data entry process.

While VEGMON provides several options for data export, researchers may want to use export formats other than those provided. Generally, the required changes can be made by modifying the final query using Access design mode. If a new query must be generated essentially from scratch, it's helpful to know that each export query is built on a parameter query that filters out records. This parameter query is linked to the user interface by way of form parameters, the values given by the form and control (combo box) names. There are just two parameters: time and location. Time may be indicated by 'year' or by 'SamplingPeriodID'. Location is always indicated by 'LocationID'. As always, make a back-up copy of the database before modifying its functionality.

VII. Version Control

Version control provides a logical organization for database archives, it helps prevent data overwrites and it ensures that only the most current copy of the database will be used in any analysis.

Versions of archived data sets are handled by adding a floating point number to the file name, with the first version being numbered 1.0. Each major version is assigned a sequentially higher whole number. Each minor version is assigned a sequentially higher .1 number. Major version changes include migrations across Access releases and complete rebuilds of front-ends and analysis tools. Minor version changes include bug fixes in front-end and analysis tools.

Prior to any major changes of a data set, a copy should be stored with the appropriate version number. This allows for the tracking of changes over time. Notify frequent users of database version updates, previous archives and their locations.

VIII. Backups

Secure data archiving is essential for protecting data files from corruption. HTLN maintains an SOP for backing up two program servers. One server is located at the Missouri State University (MSU) campus and the other at the visitor's center at Wilson's Creek National Battlefield (WICR). Both servers are Dell PowerEdge 2950 IIIs with minor differences in configuration. Backups are made to large external hard drives.

A complete backup of each system should be made at least once a week. System backups should be stored off-site. Project files and databases should be exchanged between the two servers at least once per month. Files are exchanged using a portable hard drive. Files are synchronized between servers based on file size and most recent date modified. Server comparisons are made using Beyond Compare, Scooter Software, Inc. For greater security, files from MSU should be read-only at WICR and files from WICR should be read-only at MSU. In addition, files from each location should be handled in separate directories on the transfer hard drive.

IX. Metadata

Up-to-date metadata are a requirement for Natural Resource Inventory and Monitoring databases and a requirement of federally funded databases in general. Fortunately, there are some excellent metadata tools that have been developed by Natural Resource WASO staff. "NPS Metadata Tools and Extractor" or the equivalent should be used to create VEGMON metadata to meet FGDC requirements. Metadata for VEGMON should be provided to the NPS Natural Resources GIS Data Store or any other NPS data clearinghouses designated to manage metadata.

X.   Data Availability

VEGMON data currently do not contain distribution information for federally listed species. Never-the-less, all QA/QC steps should be completed prior to distribution of database copies. User interfaces and export queries should be tested to make sure they work before making the data publicly available. Complete metadata should always accompany copies of data. Data can be shipped either by ftp or by mailing CDs. Publicly available documents that are part of the project may be useful to those requesting data. In most instances, the user can be directed to the HTLN website where most of these documents are located.

Vegetation Community Monitoring Protocol
For the Heartland Inventory and Monitoring Network

Version 2.0 (May 2008)

Revision History Log:

Prev. Version #	Revision Date	Author	Changes Made	Reason for Change	New Version #
1.0	5/2008	K. James & L. Morrison	Revised section A and B	New method for using nested frequency data, trend analysis	2.0

This standard operating procedure (SOP) gives step-by-step instructions for summary and analysis of vegetation community monitoring data. Microsoft Access 2007 is the software environment for vegetation data management. The data summaries and analyses in this SOP provide the basic working foundation for further analyses specific to a national park unit. This SOP forms the core data analysis for vegetation monitoring data while individual reports will build on the data summaries described below. Additional statistical analyses that are park-, community-, or objective-specific will be detailed in the methods section of the individual reports. This SOP is divided into two sections: Section A – Data Summary and Section B – Community Change Detection. Section A provides details on: 1) determining species abundance and frequency, 2) describing community diversity at the study unit or park level, 3) describing species diversity at the site level, 4) defining core species and optimized frequency, 5) estimating abundance of plant guilds, 6) calculating density and basal area of overstory trees in forested communities and 7) calculating tree regeneration in forested communities. These parameters should be analyzed each time a survey is completed. Section B provides details on long-term trend analyses. Trend analyses will be used to examine a select suite of robust plant community metrics and indices across time.

I. Section A – Data Summary

Plant Community Data Summaries: The plant community variables and indices selected for data summary were designed to provide resource managers with easily interpretable and timely feedback to assist in assessing management practices (Pickett *et al.* 1992). The monitoring site is used as the unit of replication and plots within sites are pooled or averaged. Once estimates for all parameters have been obtained for each site, averages and standard deviations among sites can then be obtained for individual study units (management units or reference frames) or for park-wide inferences. Numbered subsections below reflect the order in which data summaries and analyses should be conducted.

1) Individual Species Abundance and Frequency Summaries: For all species, in both prairie and forested communities, individual abundance and frequency are calculated at the monitoring site level. It is from these two metrics that all subsequent data summaries and analyses are generated.

Foliar cover serves as an estimate of abundance for herbaceous species. Foliar cover class interval data are converted to median percent values to estimate percent cover for each herbaceous and shrub species. Mean percent foliar cover at a site is calculated from all 10 m^2 plots within the site. Species frequency at a site is calculated as the proportion (or percentage) of 10 m^2 plots in which the species occurs. Thus, for each monitoring site, each species sampled has a percent foliar cover value and a frequency percentage associated with it.

2) Community Diversity Analysis: Three community diversity metrics are calculated at the study unit or park-wide level to provide an overview of compositional heterogeneity across the area of interest (Whittaker 1972). All three measures of community diversity are based on species presence/absence within and among monitoring sites. **Alpha diversity** is calculated as the average species richness per site. The total number of distinct species among all monitoring sites within the area of interest (study unit or park-wide) is the **gamma diversity**.

> alpha = average species richness among monitoring sites
> gamma = total number of distinct species across all monitoring sites
> beta = (gamma/alpha) - 1

Beta diversity, a measure of heterogeneity in the community, is calculated as the ratio of gamma diversity to alpha diversity minus one. Each metric provides a different measure of species diversity in the community. Although beta diversity is a unit-less metric, it is an informal indicator of how many distinct communities are present in the study unit or park. In general, beta values <1 are low and >5 are considered high, with beta = 0 indicating all sites contain the same species (zero variation in species composition among sites) (McCune and Grace 2002).

3) Species Diversity Analysis: Individual species abundance data are used to derive species diversity metrics at the site level.

Species richness (S) is the total number of plant taxa recorded per site. Species richness is calculated with all species (native and exotic) included in the estimate.

The **Shannon diversity index** (H') is calculated for each site as:

$$H' = - \sum_{i=1}^{n} p_i \ln p_i$$

where p_i is the relative cover of species i (Shannon 1948).

Species distribution evenness (J') is calculated by site according to Pielou (1977):

$$J' = H' / \ln(S)$$

where H' is the Shannon index and ln(S) is the maximum possible Shannon diversity for a given number of species if all species were present in equal numbers. Evenness is a measure of distribution of species within a community as compared to equal distribution and maximum diversity (Pielou 1969).

Simpson's index of diversity for an infinite population (D) is calculated by site (McCune and Grace 2002). It is the likelihood that two randomly chosen individuals from a site will be different species, emphasizing common species (McCune and Grace 2002). It is calculated using the complement of Simpson's original index of dominance:

$$\text{Simpson's index of diversity} = 1 - \sum_{i}^{n} p_i^2$$

Shannon and Simpson's index values are converted into effective number of species for each community (H_e and D_e, respectively). This allows for both diversity measures to be compared directly to species richness of the sites (S) within and among sample years based on counts of distinct species in the community (Jost 2006).

The **effective number of species based on the Shannon index** (H_e) is calculated using the following formula:

$$H_e = e^{(H')}$$

where H' is the Shannon index value.

The **effective number of species based on Simpson's index of diversity** (D_e) is the inverse of the index value or:

$$D_e = 1/(1-D)$$

where D is the Simpson's index of diversity value.

When interested in measuring diversity in a single community, it is best to use all three diversity measures to most accurately reflect diversity (Jost 2006). At the most basic level of species diversity, species richness provides a total number of distinct species sampled per unit area. Richness is insensitive to species abundance. Therefore a species with one individual occurring in a community is treated the same as a species with thousands of individuals in the community. The Shannon index (H') weights species by their abundance. The Shannon number (H_e) is the equivalent number of species with equal abundance. It is intermediate between species richness and Simpson's index in its sensitivity to rare species. Therefore this diversity measure provides information on both the count of unique species and their abundance in the community. Simpson's index goes one step further by disproportionately favoring dominant species based on species abundance and is little affected by gain or loss of rare species.

Dominance takes into account species abundance and evenness of distribution in the community. The degree of species abundance and dominance in the community is reflected by the degree to which $S > H_e > D_e$ when evenness (J') remains stable in a single community. The difference in number of species between the diversity measures reflects the presence of uncommon species and how species diversity is partitioned within the community. If all species occur in equal abundance in the community within and among sample years, then $S = H_e = D_e$. Effective number of species for each diversity measure reflects the number of species found in a similar community when all species occur in equal abundance. For example, if $S = 100$ and $D_e = 20$, then the community is dominated by 20 species and 80 species occur in low abundance. Such a community would be equivalent to a community with just 20 species all occurring in equal abundance.

Reporting effective number of species for each measure of diversity provides an intuitive method of reporting all three diversity measures within and among years in a single figure (e.g., Figure 12. 1). This method illustrates the species diversity components within and among sites for each sample year.

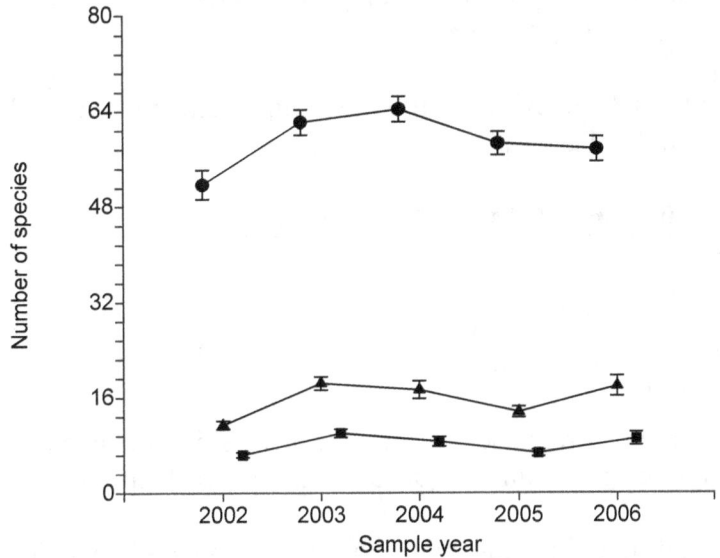

Figure 12.1. Species richness (circle) and effective number of species for two diversity measures (Shannon's index, triangle; and Simpson's index, square) for sites (n = 18) across sample years. Symbol is the mean and error bars are ± 1 standard error of the mean. (from Tallgrass Prairie National Preserve).

4) Optimized Frequency of Abundant Species: For abundant species (i.e. >15% frequency at the 10 m^2 scale), tracking changes in optimized frequency is a good surrogate for measuring plant density. Optimized frequency is most sensitive to changes in underlying density. A plot frame size that delivers a species' optimized frequency is referred to as the optimal plot. Size of the optimal plot decreases as density, and the spatial structure of local density, increases (Heywood and DeBacker 2007). Population simulation work demonstrated a plot frame size that returned a mean frequency from 20% to 50% is most sensitive for detecting changes in the underlying density of populations over time across a broad range of spatial structure (Heywood and DeBacker 2007). Optimized frequency is determined for each abundant species.

Optimized frequency is determined after data collection has occurred and prior to the analysis phase. SOP #5 describes how species occurrence data are collected from the smallest to largest plots. Accordingly, for all species at each of the ten sampling plots within the site, there are four possible frequency scenarios that can be encountered (below and Table 12.1):

- Species A is encountered in the smallest plot frame (0.01 m^2), recorded as a '1' for that plot frame and also for all three larger frames (0.1 m^2, 1 m^2 and 10 m^2) in which it is nested. Thus Species A is present in all four nested plot frames.
- Species B is encountered in the 0.1 m^2 plot frame for which a '1' is recorded for that plot frame and also for the two larger frames (1 m^2 and 10 m^2) in which it is nested. Thus Species B is present in the three larger nested plot frames.
- Species C is encountered in the 1 m^2 plot frame for which a '1' is recorded for that plot frame and also for the next larger 10 m^2 frame in which it is nested. Thus Species C is present in the two largest nested plot frames.
- Species D is encountered only in the 10 m^2 plot frame for which a '1' is recorded for that plot frame only. Thus Species D is present only in the largest plot frame and not recorded in any of the smaller nested plot frames.

Table 12.1. Four species tallied according to the first individual encountered in the nested plot frames for a single plot within a site.

Site	Plot	Species	0.01 m^2	0.1 m^2	1 m^2	10 m^2
1	10A	Species A	1	1	1	1
1	10A	Species B	0	1	1	1
1	10A	Species C	0	0	1	1
1	10A	Species D	0	0	0	1

Once all species have been tallied, frequency of each species (%) is calculated for each plot frame size yielding four species-plot frame frequency values for each species.

Species are assigned to a plot frame size that yields, on average over all years (or baseline year(s)) a frequency near 35% (Table 12.2). Note – these analyses are not appropriate if species abundances are changing substantially from year to year so that a different plot frame size is needed among years to yield an optimized frequency measure. Once assigned an optimal plot, frequency is calculated from that same plot frame size each year of the study. The proportion of optimal plots in which the species occurrs is defined as the species' optimized frequency.

Table 12.2 Species frequency calculated at four plot frame sizes at Tallgrass Prairie National Preserve. The plot frame size yielding an optimized frequency value shown in grey.

ScientificName	Plot Frame Size			
	0.01 m²	0.1 m²	1 m²	10 m²
Andropogon gerardii	62.2%	91.8%	97.1%	99.1%
Schizachyrium scoparium	49.9%	80.6%	92.1%	98.2%
Bouteloua curtipendula	43.1%	74.0%	86.1%	94.3%
Sporobolius asper	5.4%	25.2%	61.4%	85.0%
Sorghastrum nutans	10.6%	28.2%	54.6%	84.7%
Panicum virgatum	9.9%	34.8%	60.8%	84.0%
Aster ericoides	7.8%	33.1%	59.7%	76.2%
Eragrostis spectabilis	4.1%	16.0%	42.4%	70.6%
Ambrosia psilostachya	6.2%	24.3%	43.4%	52.0%
Amphiachyris dracunculoides	2.2%	12.4%	30.7%	51.4%
Amorpha canescens	4.7%	15.8%	34.7%	51.0%
Dichanthelium spp	2.8%	13.3%	26.9%	42.1%
Bouteloua hirsuta	7.7%	19.2%	28.3%	39.7%
Carex spp	8.6%	19.3%	28.4%	38.3%
Digitaria cognata	1.1%	4.1%	13.7%	34.9%
Buchloe dactyloides	3.8%	8.2%	16.3%	32.9%
Ruellia humilis	0.6%	5.0%	14.9%	30.1%
Chamaesyce prostrata	0.3%	4.3%	13.1%	28.4%
Vernonia baldwinii	0.3%	1.8%	8.6%	27.1%
Bouteloua gracilis	3.2%	7.2%	12.9%	24.1%
Dalea purpurea	0.3%	3.1%	8.0%	24.1%
Salvia azurea	0.3%	1.9%	7.7%	23.6%
Linum sulcatum	0.7%	2.3%	8.3%	22.1%
Aster oblongifolius	0.2%	2.4%	7.9%	19.9%
Solidago missouriensis	0.8%	3.9%	8.7%	19.6%
Brickellia eupatorioides	0.0%	0.4%	5.0%	17.4%
Artemisia ludoviciana	0.3%	2.3%	5.7%	16.4%

Optimized frequency data allows for tracking changes in the density of individual species (Figure 12.2), or for comparing trends in optimized frequency among species (Figure 12.3). Differences in optimized frequency of all abundant species from one time period to another indicates the general trajectory and amplitude of change (Figure 12.4) (National Park Service, Michael DeBacker, unpublished results, 2009).

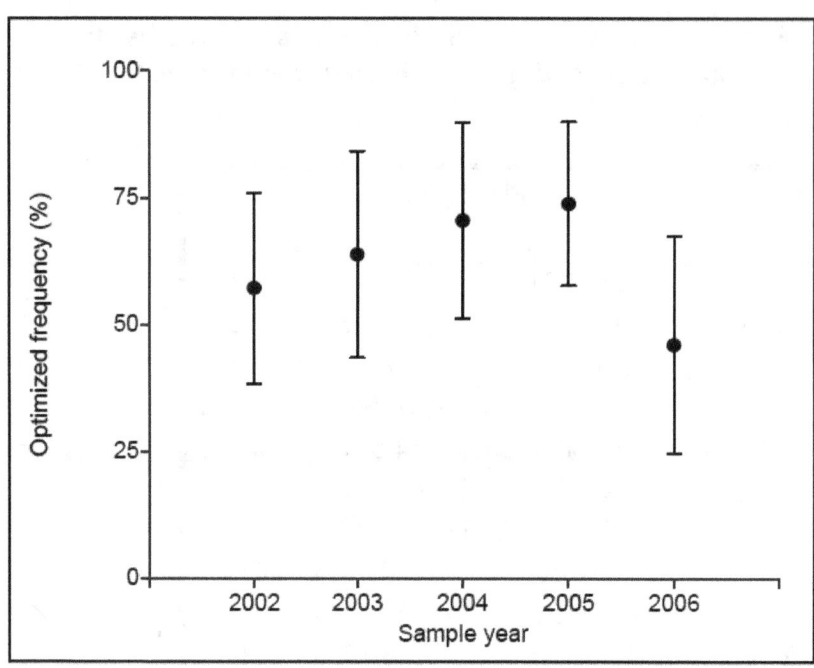

Figure 12.2. Site mean (±1 standard deviation) optimized frequency (0.01 m² plot frame size) for *Andropogon gerardii* (Big bluestem) among sample years at Tallgrass Prairie National Preserve (TAPR).

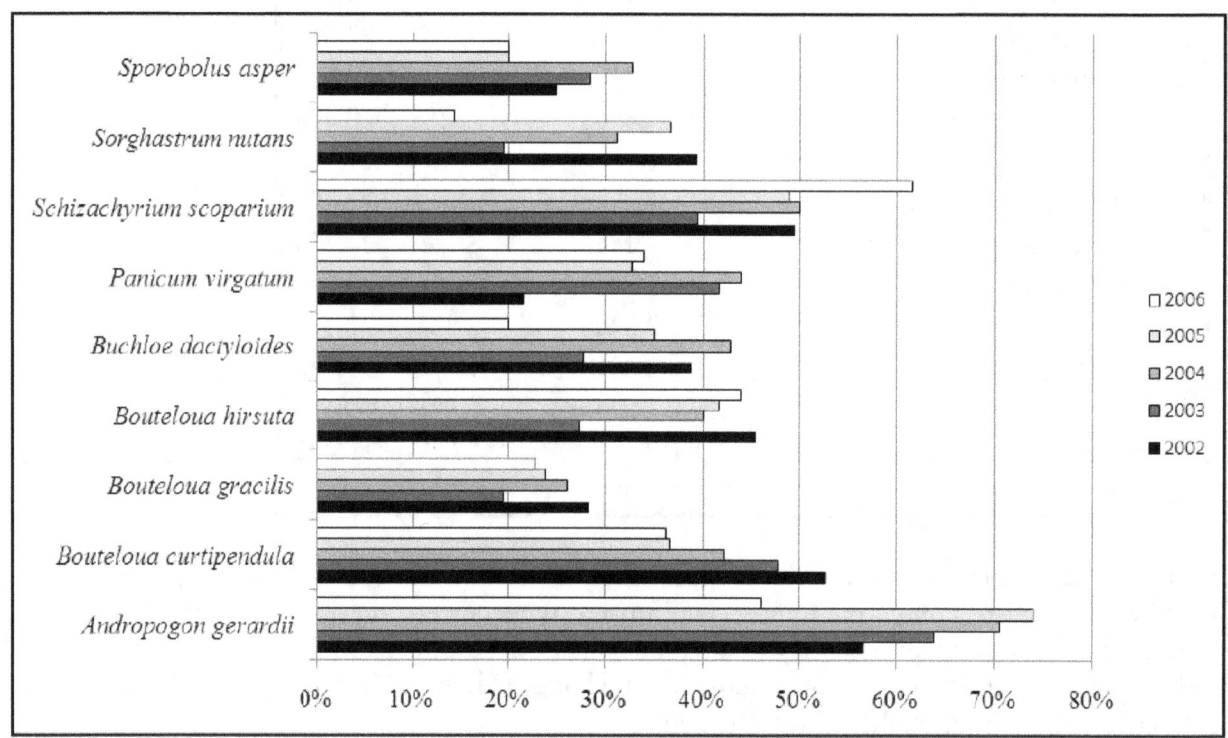

Figure 12.3. Optimized frequency for eight warm season grass species at Tallgrass Prairie National Preserve (TAPR).

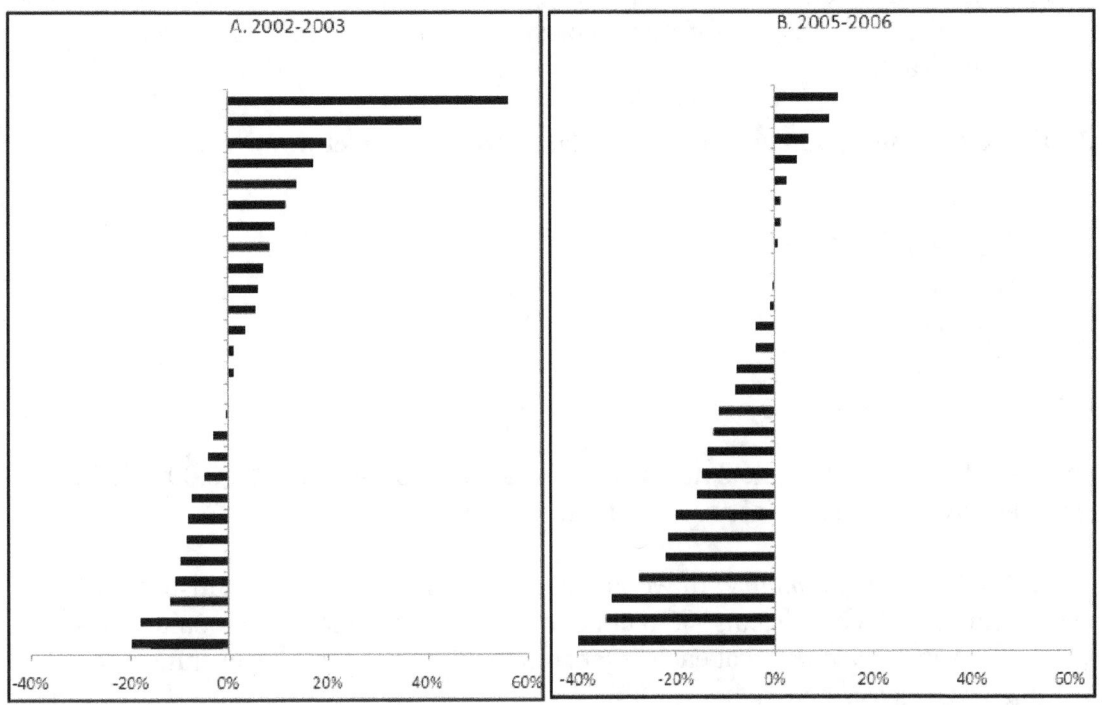

Figure 12.4 Distribution of inter-annual changes in optimized frequency for 27 species: A) 2002 to 2003, B) 2005 to 2006, at Tallgrass Prairie National Preserve (TAPR).

5) Prairie Plant Guild and Exotic Species Summary: Frequency, average cover and associated standard deviation are also calculated for 10 plant guilds: warm-season grasses, cool-season grasses, annuals and biennials, ephemeral spring forbs, spring forbs, summer/fall forbs, legumes, ferns, woody species (shrubs) and grass-like species. Ecological prairie plant guilds are composed of species with significant overlap in niche requirements and that occupy similar positions along a resource gradient in a community (Root 1967, Kindscher and Wells 1995). Summary information by guilds is useful for interpreting the type and quality of prairie, as well as detecting compositional shifts among guilds that might result from management. Median values of foliar cover classes for species belonging to each guild are summed within the 10 m^2 plot frame and then averaged for the entire site to provide a guild cover value at the monitoring site level.

Exotic species form a different type of species guild, specific to species intentionally or unintentionally introduced into an area outside of their natural range. Exotic species can influence ecological processes including trophic level relationships, interspecific competition, primary and secondary succession, nutrient cycling and ecosystem productivity, diversity and stability (Bratton 1982). Three metrics are calculated for exotic species for each site: 1) mean ratio of exotic plant species to total number of native plant species, 2) frequency and 3) mean cover of exotic species.

6) Overstory Data Summary: In woodland communities, summary statistics for overstory tree species (stems ≥ 5.0 cm dbh) are calculated for each monitoring site and averaged for each study unit. For each species, density and basal area are calculated. Density, or the number of stems per sample unit, is a measure of abundance for tree species. Overstory density is calculated for five size classes (cm dbh) (Table 12.3).

Table 12.3. Diameter at breast height (cm) size class ranges for overstory trees.

Size Class	dbh (cm)
1	5 - 14.9
2	15 - 24.9
3	25 - 34.9
4	35 - 44.9
5 45+	

Basal area by size class (m^2/ha) is calculated using the standard formula, dbh^2 x 0.00007854. Basal area and density data are summarized for the study unit.

7) Seedling and Sapling Data Summary: In woodland communities, summary statistics for seedlings and sapling tree species (stems < 5.0 cm dbh) are calculated for each monitoring site. For each species, density is calculated at each regeneration size class. Tree regeneration density is reported in three size classes (cm dbh):

- seedlings (stems < 0.5 m in height)
- small saplings (stems ≥ 0.5 m in height but < 2.5 cm dbh)
- large saplings (stems ≥ 2.5 cm dbh but < 5.0 cm dbh)

Total density is also reported by summing over the tree regeneration size classes.

II. Section B – Community Change Detection

Scope of Analyses: It will not usually be necessary or desirable to conduct long-term analyses for change on all data recorded. Indeed, this protocol produces a very large amount of information and the amount of staff time and resources that potentially could be spent summarizing and analyzing the various variables far exceeds that available. Thus a subset of the variables will be selected for specific analyses relative to park vegetation communities and management objectives. The focus is on temporal and spatial change in community composition and structure and how it is related to environmental and management measurements.

Analyses for community change detection should begin with the relatively simple approaches described below (exploratory analyses, parameter estimation and control charts) and progress to more complicated analyses when biologically important changes seem to be occurring and the simpler analyses do not yield all the necessary information. The approaches are listed roughly from the simple to the more complex.

Exploratory Analyses: Exploratory data analyses are relatively straightforward and include graphs such as scatter plots, frequency histograms and box plots (see Elzinga et al. 2001 for some examples). Such graphs are simple to construct and easy to understand. The construction of the relevant graphs for the parameters of interest should always be the first step in any long-term analysis. Biologically important change will usually be obvious from the graphed data and such graphical depictions may be useful in suggesting any potential additional statistical tests. Such graphical techniques will also allow one to assess the assumptions on which various statistical tests are based and screen for outliers.

Parameter Estimation: Parameter estimation involves simply providing the best estimate of the parameter of interest at each time interval. Some measure of the amount of uncertainty associated with this estimate should also be provided. This may be in the form of standard deviations, standard errors, or confidence intervals, depending upon the primary information one wishes to convey. Usually confidence intervals will supply the most useful information about the location of a particular parameter. Confidence intervals of 90 or 95% are common. The percentage should depend upon the amount of uncertainty one is willing to accept relative to the need for a precise interval.

Confidence intervals based on the Student's *t*-distribution are described in elementary statistics texts. It should be noted that the construction of a confidence interval based on the Student's *t* distribution assumes the data are from a normal distribution. If the data are not normal, the confidence interval will be approximate rather than exact. Non-parametric confidence intervals may also be constructed, although these are usually very wide and thus less sensitive to change (Conover 1999). Care must be taken in interpretation of confidence intervals; they are frequently misinterpreted when making comparisons (see Cumming et al. 2004, Belia et al. 2005, Cumming and Finch 2005).

Control Charts: The construction and interpretation of control charts is covered in many texts focusing on quality control in industry (*e.g.*, Beauregard et al. 1992, Gyrna 2001, Montgomery 2001). The application of control charts for ecological purposes, however, is relatively straightforward. The use of control charts in environmental monitoring is discussed in texts by McBean and Rovers (1998) and Manly (2001), although not in as great detail as the texts referenced above focusing on industrial applications. Many different types of control charts could be constructed, depending upon the type of information desired. For example, control charts can be used to evaluate variables or attributes (*i.e.*, count or frequency data) and focus on measures of central tendency or dispersion.

Most traditional control charts assume that observations come from a normal distribution, or that data can be transformed to normality. In industry, control limits are often set at a distance of 3 standard deviations on either side of the centerline (Wetherill and Brown 1991, Beauregard et al. 1992, Montgomery 2001). Thus, assuming a normal distribution centered at the centerline, the control limits would encompass 99.73 % of the distribution. Control limits may be constructed so as to contain any desired proportion of the distribution (i.e., representing $[1-\alpha]$ confidence intervals for any α). In this case, choosing control limits is equivalent to specifying a critical region for testing the hypothesis that a specific observation is statistically different from the proposed centerline value. (It is crucial that the centerline value is representative of the true population parameter.) Control limits could also be based on probabilistic thresholds other than confidence intervals (e.g., McBean and Rovers 1998). If the observations cannot be assumed to come from a normal distribution, it is possible to construct control charts based on other distributions (*e.g.*, a Poisson distribution as in Atkinson et al. 2003) and construct analogous confidence limits, as long as the distributions are known.

It is not absolutely necessary to use values from a statistical sampling process to determine centerlines and thresholds for action. It is possible to subjectively choose a centerline value as the desired state and set threshold limits to match the amount of variability with which one is comfortable for the variable of interest. It is crucial to realize that this approach has no statistical basis and thus probabilities cannot be readily associated with the observations. This application also has a precedent in industry. Such charts, which plot observations without relevance to an underlying distribution, have been termed 'conformance charts'. Threshold values, which may be subjective, are termed 'action limits' (Beauregard et al. 1992). If taking this approach, one should be very familiar with the system in question and preferably select values that are defensible based on the data.

Although control charts have potentially wide applicability, each application may be different. A generic process for control chart construction is provided below, although decisions will always have to be made and an analyst familiar with control charts should ideally be consulted.

Steps in constructing a univariate control chart (Figure 12.5):

1. Determine the parameter of interest. This could be practically any variable or index derived from this protocol.

2. After several years of data are available, plot the values of the parameter of interest (on the y-axis) against time (on the x-axis).

3. Determine a "center-line" value for this parameter; this could represent a mean of the observations, a target value, or some other value. Determining an appropriate center-line contains inherent pitfalls and an analyst who is familiar with control charts should be consulted.

4. Establish control limits around the center-line. It is possible that only an upper control limit, or only a lower control limit, or both will be necessary, depending upon the parameter of interest and management concerns. Control limits may be based on a probability distribution and thus allow one to make statistical inferences, or they may be based on target levels set by management. Once again, determining appropriate control limits can be tricky, especially if statistical inferences are desired and an analyst who is familiar with control charts should be consulted.

5. Continue to plot values of the parameter of interest over time as new data become available. If an observation exceeds the control limit(s), this is indicative of the potential need for management action, or a more focused study.

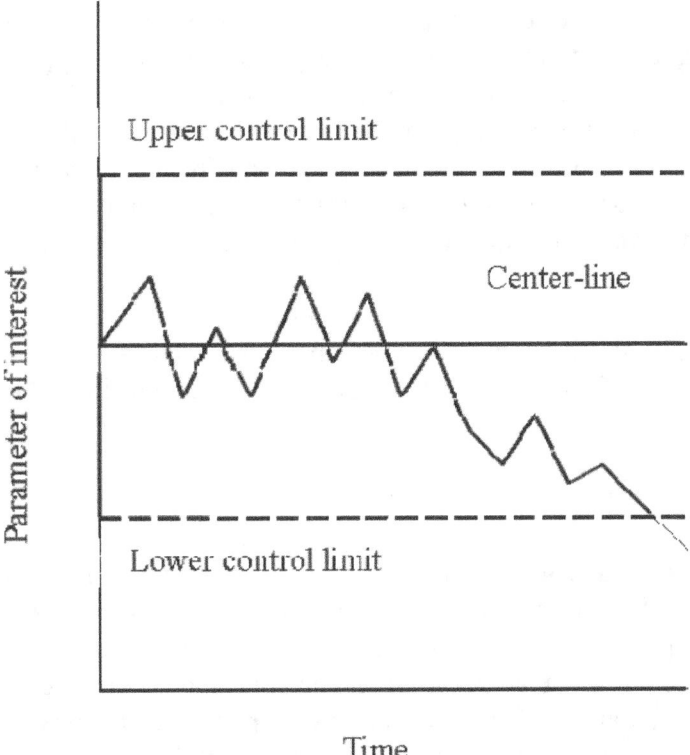

Figure 12.5. Generic univariate control chart.

Simple Statistical Tests: Simple statistical tests could be used to test for differences in variables between years. The paired *t*-test is used with non-proportional variables such as species richness and tree species density and is appropriate for permanent plots. The non-parametric Wilcoxon signed rank test can also be used to test non-proportional variables for differences between years (Elzinga et al. 2001). The non-parametric McNemar's test can be used with proportional variables such as mean percent cover and exotic: native species ratio.

Regression and ANOVA: Regression analyses represent an obvious method for analyzing long-term trends. It should be kept in mind, however, that regressions do not test for trend *per se*; they evaluate how well the data fit a specified function. Thus, the first step is to visually examine scatter plots of data for the most appropriate regression function. In general, three types of regression may be useful: linear, curvilinear and piecewise. See Kutner et al. (2005) for an in-depth treatment of regression models. The most informative approach to a regression analysis is likely to be estimation of regression parameters (e.g., the slope, which is indicative of the rate of change), rather than simple determination of statistical significance (because *P*-values are dependent on sample size).
Analysis of variance (ANOVA) could also be used for these data. A repeated measures design would be appropriate given that the same plots are sampled over time. This approach would be most powerful in looking at different 'treatments' (i.e., different management regimes) rather than simply looking at overall change.

Because the same plots are sampled repeatedly over time, more elaborate designs may be able to detect more subtle changes. For example, a repeated measures linear regression model (*e.g.*, Lexica and Steele 1996) could be employed. This method may be an improvement on designs assuming yearly random sampling of sites, because re-sampling the same plots theoretically reduces between-year variation. This effect will be most pronounced for long-lived perennials and patterns of variability among sites and years may need to be evaluated to determine the benefits of such an approach, relative to the added complexity of analysis and interpretation.

Data Transformation and First Difference of Time Series: Species abundance data that are obtained from fixed monitoring sites repeatedly sampled over time can be analyzed as differences, rather than raw abundance. The difference in species abundance within a site can be calculated between two sample years:

$$d_{ij} = x_{ij2} - x_{ij1}$$

where x_{ij} is the abundance of species *j* in site *i* at sample year 1 and 2. For community change it is possible to ordinate species abundance differences between sample times. For each species within a site the difference is the change in abundance through time. This "first difference" refers to the first derivative in a time series curve (Allen et al. 1977) and is the continuous equivalent of the discrete difference described above. The dataset of first differences in species abundance between two sampling events represents the changes in species composition within and among sites. Determining the difference in species abundance with each successive sampling event is indicative of the rate of compositional change across all sample years.

To analyze the transformed community difference dataset it is important to use multivariate statistical tests that allow for nonnegative numbers (McCune and Grace, 2002). These transformed data work well with tests that require multivariate normal data and linear relationships (i.e., Principal Components Analysis as conducted in PC-ORD software, McCune and Mefford 1999).

Multivariate Tests: The Multi-Response Permutation Procedure (MRPP) is a nonparametric method that uses multivariate data to test for differences between groups (Zimmerman et al. 1985, McCune and Grace 2002). The MRPP is similar to the two sample *t*-test and the one-way analysis of variance *F*-test and it can be shown to be functionally identical to these tests, as well as the Mann-Whitney Wilcoxon and other nonparametric tests (Zimmerman et al. 1985). An important advantage of MRPP is that it does not assume the data are from a normal population, or that there are homogeneous variances. MRPP analyses can be conducted with PC-ORD software (McCune and Mefford 1999).

MRPP example from Tallgrass Prairie National Preserve (TAPR):

> Differences among sites within pasture for each sample year were minimal as
> indicated by similar within-pasture distance values (Table 12.4). Greater distance
> values indicate greater differences in species composition among sites within
> pastures. In terms of species composition, sites both within and among pastures

overlapped considerably, as indicated by the small within-group agreement (A) values.

Table 12.4. Multi-response permutation procedure (MRPP) results for core sites. Average within-pasture distance measure is shown for each pasture for each year; the chance-corrected within-group agreement (A) among pastures and its P-value are shown for each year. Bold values are significant differences among pastures for that sample year at the P < 0.05 level.

Year	Crusher Hill Pasture	Red House Pasture	Gas House Pasture	Windmill Pasture	A	P-value
2002	0.291	0.308	0.335	0.339	0.0067	0.356
2003	0.343	0.312	0.288	0.358	0.0427	0.072
2004	0.313	0.288	0.287	0.353	0.0542	**0.025**
2005	0.353	0.335	0.313	0.35	0.0092	0.325
2006	0.338	0.33	0.32	0.359	0.0349	0.084

The multi-response permutation procedure resulted in only a single statistically significant result (bold value, Table 3). In 2004, the observed A was statistically different from expected, while within-group heterogeneity remained similar to all other sample years. Furthermore, the chance-corrected within-group agreement (A) values were all close to zero, indicating that species heterogeneity of sites within pastures was not different from that expected by chance alone.

Caveats of statistical tests: Before any statistical tests are conducted, data should be examined for assumptions (when applicable) such as normality and homoscedasticity (homogeneity of variances). If raw data are not normally distributed, a transformation should be considered. A $\log_{10}$ transformation will often make a data set more normal, but one should not assume such a transformation will always work. Other transformations are possible (see Kutner et al. 2005). After transformations, the distributions of the transformed data should always be examined. A formal test for normality is available and other tests can be used to evaluate other statistical assumptions, such as Bartlett's test for the existence of homoscedasticity (Sokal and Rohlf 1995).

One must be cautious in the interpretation of *P*-values from multiple tests conducted on the same data set. When more than one statistical test is conducted from the same data set, the probability of the Type I error is no longer equal to the *P*-value specified in any given test. *P*-values can be corrected for multiple comparisons (*e.g.*, the sequential Bonferroni technique, Rice 1989), albeit at a loss of statistical power (Nakagawa 2004). The more multiple comparisons made and corrected for in this way, the lower the chance of obtaining any 'significant' result. There is much debate over the appropriate method of dealing with the uncertainty of Type I errors in the context of multiple comparisons (*e.g.*, Perneger 1998, Cabin and Mitchell 2000, Moran 2003); the best strategy is to make as few multiple comparisons (*i.e.*, report as few *P*-values) as possible and to remember that the primary goal of these analyses is to detect changes before it is too late to react efficiently to undesirable changes.

III. Literature Cited

Allen, T.F.H., S.M. Bartell and J.F. Koonce. 1977. Multiple stable configurations in ordination of phytoplankton community change rates. Ecology 58: 1076-1084.

Atkinson, A. J., R. N. Fisher, C. J. Rochester and C. W. Brown. 2003. Sampling design optimization and establishment of baselines for herptofauna arrays at the Point Loma Ecological Reserve. United States Geological Survey, Western Ecological Research Center, Sacramento, CA, 39 pp.

Belia, S., Fidler, F., Williams, J. and Cumming, G. 2005. Researchers misunderstand confidence intervals and standard error bars. Psychological Methods 10: 389-396.

Beauregard, M. R., R. J. Mikulak and B. A. Olson. 1992. A practical guide to statistical quality improvement: Opening up the statistical toolbox. Van Nostrand Reinhold, New York, NY.

Bratton, S.P. 1982. The effects of exotic plant and animal species on nature preserves. Natural Areas Journal 2: 3 – 13.

Cabin, R.J. and Mitchell, R.J. 2000. To Bonferroni or not to Bonferroni: When and how are the questions. Bulletin of the Ecological Society of America 81: 246-248.

Collins, S.L. and S.M. Glenn. 1990. A hierarchical analysis of species abundance patterns in grassland vegetation. American Naturalist 135: 633 – 648.

Conover, W. J. 1999. Practical Nonparametric Statistics. John Wiley & Sons, Inc., New York, NY.

Cumming, G. and Finch, S. 2005. Inference by eye: Confidence intervals and how to read pictures of data. American Psychologist 60: 170-180.

Cumming, G., Williams, J. and Fidler, F. 2004. Replication and researchers' understanding of confidence intervals and standard error bars. Understanding Statistics 3: 299-311.

Elzinga, C.L., D.W. Salzer, J.W. Willoughby and J.P. Gibbs. 2001. Monitoring Plant and Animal Populations. Blackwell Science, Malden, MA.

Gyrna, F. M. 2001. Quality planning and analysis: From product development through use. McGraw-Hill Irwin, New York, NY.

Heywood, J.S. and M.D. DeBacker. 2007. Optim al Sam pling Designs for Monitoring P lant Frequency. Rangeland Ecology and Management 60(4).

Jost, L. 2006. Entropy and Divesity. Oikos 113:2.

Kindscher, K. and P.V. Wells. 1995. Prairie plant guilds: a multivariate analysis of prairie plan t species based on ecological and morphological traits. Vegetatio 117: 29 – 50.

Kutner, M. H., C. J. Nachtsheim, J. Neter and W. Li. 2005. Applied Linear Statistical Models. McGraw Hill Irwin, Boston, MA.

Lesica, P. and B.M. Steele. 1996. A method for monitoring long-term population trends: an example using rare arctic-alpine plants. Ecological Applications 6: 879 – 887.

Manly, B. F. J. 2001. Statistics for environmental science and management. Chapman & Hall/CRC, Boca Raton, FL.

McBean, E. A. and F. A. Rovers. 1998. Statistical procedures for analysis of environmental monitoring data and risk assessment. Prentice Hall PTR, Upper Saddle River, NJ.

McCune, B. and J. B. Grace. 2002. Analysis of Ecological Communities. MJM software Design.

McCune, B. and M.J. Mefford. 1999. PC-ORD. Multivariate Analysis of Ecological Data, Version 4. MjM Software Design, Gleneden Beach, Oregon, USA.

Montgomery, D. C. 2001. Introduction to statistical quality control. John Wiley & Sons, Inc, New York, NY.

Moran, M.D. 2003. Arguments for rejecting the sequential Bonferroni in ecological studies. Oikos 100: 403-405.

Nakagawa, S. 2004. A farewell to Bonferroni: the problems of low statistical power and publication bias. Behavioral Ecology 15: 1044-10445.

Perneger, T.V. 1998. What's wrong with Bonferroni adjustments. British Medical Journal 316: 1236-1238.

Pickett, S.T.A., V.T. Parker and P.T. Fiedler. 1992. The new paradigm in ecology: implications for conservation biology above the species level. Pages 65-88 in P.L. Fiedler and S.K. Jain (editors) Conservation Biology: The Theory and Practice of Conservation, Preservation and Management. Chapman and Hall, New York, New York. 507pp.

Pielou, E.C. 1977. Population and Community Ecology. New York: Gordon and Breach.

Rice, W.R. 1989. Analyzing tables of statistical tests. Evolution 43: 223-225.

Root, R.B. 1967. The niche exploitation pattern of the blue-gray gnatcatcher. Ecological Monographs 37: 317 – 350.

Shannon, C.E. 1948 A Mathematical Theory of Communication. Reprinted with corrections from The Bell System Technical Journal, Vol. 27, pp. 379-423, 623-656, July, October 1948.

Sokal, R.R. and F.J. Rohlf. 1995. Biometry, 3rd edition. W.H. Freeman and Co. New York. 887 pp.

Wetherill, G.B. and Brown, D.W. 1991. Statistical Process Control: Theory and Practice. London, Chapman & Hall.

Whittaker, R. H. 1972. Evolution and measurement of species diversity. Taxon 21: 213-251.

Zimmerman, G.M., H. Goetz and P.W. Mielke, Jr. 1985. Use of an improved statistical method for group comparisons to study effects of prairie fire. Ecology 66:606-611.

**Vegetation Community Monitoring Protocol
For the Heartland Inventory and Monitoring Network**

Standard Operating Procedure 13: Reporting and Presentation

Version 2.00 (July 2009)

Revision History Log:

Prev. Version #	Revision Date	Author	Changes Made	Reason for Change	New Version #
1.0 07/2009		D.G. Peitz K.M. James	Revise entire document	Reflect use of NRTR format	2.0

This SOP gives step-by-step instructions for reporting on vegetation community monitoring data collected by Heartland Inventory and Monitoring Network (HTLN). The SOP describes the procedure for formatting a report, the review process and distribution of completed reports. Efficient reporting on monitoring results is critical in assisting park Resource Managers in management decisions. Therefore, a reporting schedule is given with critical dates identified.

I. Report Format

Template
The report template for Natural Resource Technical Reports should be followed (http://www.nature.nps.gov/publications/NRPM/index.cfm). Natural resource reports are the designated medium for disseminating high priority, current natural resource management information with managerial application. The Natural Resource Technical Reports series is used to disseminate the peer-reviewed results of scientific studies in the physical, biological and social sciences for both the advancement of science and the achievement of the National Park Service's mission.

Style
Standards for scientific writing as recommended in the CBE Style Manual (CBE Style Manual Committee 1994) should be followed. Reports should be direct and concise. Refer also to Mack (1986), Day and Gastel (2006) and Strunk and White (2000) for guidelines on appropriate writing style.

II. Types of Reports and Review Process

Table 9.1 summarizes the types of reports produced and the review process. Adapted from DeBacker et al. 2005.

Type of Report	Purpose of Report	Primary Audience	Review Process	Frequency
Comprehensive 4 - year Status Reports	Summarize monitoring data collected during a sampling year by HTLN and any observations made by park staff and volunteers during the previous three years, to provide an update on the status of plant communities. Document related data management activities and data summaries.	Park resource managers and external scientists	Internal peer review by HTLN staff	Every 4th year
Executive Summary of Comprehensive 4 - year Status Reports	Same as Comprehensive 4 – year Status Reports but summarized to highlight key points for non-technical audiences.	Superintendents, interpreters and the general public	Internal peer review by HTLN staff	Simultaneous with Comprehensive 4 -year Status Reports
Comprehensive Trends and Analysis and Synthesis Reports	Describe and interpret trends in plant communities. Describe and interpret relationships among observed trends and park management, known stressors, climate, *etc.* Highlight resources of concern that may require management action.	Park resource managers and external scientists	Internal peer review by HTLN staff	Every 12 -16 years
Executive Summary of Comprehensive Trends and Analysis and Synthesis Reports	Same as Comprehensive Trends and Analysis and Synthesis Reports, but summarized to highlight findings and recommendations for non-technical audiences.	Superintendents, interpreters and the general public	Internal peer review by HTLN staff	Simultaneous with Comprehensive Trends Analysis and Synthesis Reports

III. Report Distribution

Following review, the comprehensive report for a park will be distributed to the resource management staff and the superintendent by the beginning of the next field season after data is collected by the HTLN. Reports can also be distributed to interested partners involved in conservation or restoration of plant communities. This determination is made by the park, the network, or the regional office. All data collected are public property and subject to requests under the Freedom of Information Act (FOIA). However, sensitive data, such as the location of rare species, must be withheld in some cases. Reports containing non-sensitive data will be made publicly available and disseminated through the network website: (http://science.nature.nps.gov/im/units/htln/).

IV.   Literature Cited

CBE Style Manual Committee. 1994. Scientific style and format: the CBE manual for authors, editors and publishers. Sixth edition. Council of Biology Editors, Cambridge University Press, New York, New York, USA.

DeBacker, M.D., C.C Young (editor), P. Adams, L. Morrison, D. Peitz, G.A. Rowell, M. Williams and D. Bowles. 2005. Heartland Inventory and Monitoring Networks and Prairie Cluster Prototype Monitoring Program Vital Signs Monitoring Plan. National Park Service, Heartland Inventory and Monitoring Networks and Prairie Cluster Prototype Monitoring Program, Wilson's Creek National Battlefield, Republic, Missouri. 104 p. plus appendices.

Day, R.A. 1983. How to write and publish a scientific paper. Second edition. ISI Press, Philadelphia, Pennsylvania, USA.

Mack, R.N. 1986. Writing with precision, clarity and economy. Bulletin of Ecological Society of America 67:31-35.

Strunk, W. Jr. and E.B. White. 1979. The Elements of Style. Third Edition. Macmillan, New York, New York, USA.

Vegetation Community Monitoring Protocol
for the Heartland Inventory and Monitoring Network

Version 1.0 (December 2004)

Revision History Log:

Previous Version #	Revision Date	Author	Changes Made	Reason for Change	New Version #

This Standard Operating Procedure explains how to make and track changes to the Vegetation Monitoring Protocol for the Heartland Inventory and Monitoring Network narrative and accompanying SOPs. Observers asked to edit the Protocol Narrative or any one of the SOPs need to follow this outlined procedure to eliminate confusion in how data are collected and analyzed. All observers should be familiar with this SOP to identify and use the most current methodologies.

I.   Procedures:

1. The Vegetation Monitoring Protocol for the Heartland Inventory and Monitoring Network (HTLN) narrative and accompanying SOPs has attempted to incorporate the soundest methodologies for collecting and analyzing vegetation community data. However, all protocols regardless of how sound require editing as new and different information becomes available. Required edits should be made in a timely manner and appropriate reviews undertaken.

2. All edits require review for clarity and technical soundness. Small changes or additions to existing methods will be reviewed in-house by HTLN staff. However, if a complete change in methods is sought, an outside review is required. Regional and national staff of the National Park Service with familiarity in plant community research and data analysis will be utilized as reviewers. Also, experts in plant community research and statistical methodologies outside of the Park Service will be utilized in the review process.

3. Document edits and protocol versioning are tracked in the Revision History Log that accompanies the Protocol Narrative and each SOP. Log changes in the Protocol Narrative or SOP being edited only. Version numbers increase incrementally, major changes by whole numbers (i.e. version 1.0, version 2.0, etc.) and minor changes by tenths (e.g. version 1.1, version 1.2, etc). Record the previous version number, date of revision, author of the revision and identify paragraphs and pages where changes are made and the reason for making the changes along with the new version number.

4. Inform the Data Manager about changes to the Protocol Narrative or SOP so the new version number can be incorporated in the Metadata of the project database. The database may have to be edited by the Data Manager to accompany changes in the Protocol Narrative and SOPs.

5. Post new versions on the internet and forward copies to all individuals with a previous version of the affected Protocol Narrative or SOP.

Appendices

Appendix A. Proposal to Change how Plant Communities are Sampled Through Time in the Heartland Network.

Kevin James, Lloyd Morrison and Mike DeBacker

Executive Summary:

Accounting for inter-annual variability between sample years is an underlying factor in the current revisit design. Furthermore, it provides a balance between sampling tours that allows for the greatest amount of field work to be accomplished per year while minimizing cost. The two-year-on, three-year-off revisit plan provides an estimate of inter-annual variability while protecting sites from trampling effects. Using a mean value across time periods reduces the effect of short-term variation. Averaging monitoring data across time periods, however, results in a loss of information by smoothing the data. Utilizing readily available datasets, it is now possible to analyze monitoring data and environmental data simultaneously to better address the short-term effects of weather on the measured response. Switching to a one-year-on, three-year-off schedule for plant community monitoring maintains all the benefits of the current logistical plan and revisit design while improving how inter-annual variability is addressed. The proposed changes to the revisit design temporally coordinate bird community, plant community and invasive plant monitoring at all parks in the network. This provides a larger window of opportunity for park managers to initiate management actions and a larger window for measurable changes to be detected in monitoring response variables. All aspects of the current sampling design will be improved as the proposed changes to the revisit design are implemented network-wide.

Introduction:

Plant community monitoring in HTLN parks consists of a logistical plan and a revisit design that is constrained by the logistical plan. The logistical plan outlines which parks are sampled during the same tour, while the revisit design is park specific and determines how the communities are sampled within and among sample years. The aim of long-term monitoring is to consistently sample communities through time so that trends in measurable changes can be detected. To accomplish the goals of long-term ecological monitoring within and among parks in the HTLN, parks must be sampled in such a manner as to maximize sampling efficiency and data quality while having the least impact on the community and program budget. The proposed changes to the logistical plan and revisit design meet these criteria while incorporating readily available environmental data to address the larger issue of inter-annual variability in monitoring data.

Currently plant community monitoring sites are measured for two consecutive years followed by a three-year interval without sampling. Sampling for two consecutive years reduces, statistically, the effect of annual variability on the detection of trends in plant communities that are temporally dynamic. Sampling a number of years consecutively and averaging across the years can provide a more precise estimate of the variable sampled than a single sample (Lesica and Steele 1996). However, this reduces the number of data points contributing to long-term trend analysis. Proper analysis of data collected under this revisit design requires the data from the two consecutive years to be averaged together and analyzed as a single data set to minimize the variability due to environmental differences between sample years.

With the availability of annual weather data and long-term climate data, it is both easy and appropriate to analyze monitoring data in conjunction with environmental data for each sample year. Accounting for inter-annual variability due to environmental differences between sample years is best done using weather (temperature and precipitation) or climate data collected at the park scale rather than averaging the monitoring data to remove variability due to environmental changes. Both weather and climate datasets are readily available and easy to analyze in conjunction with monitoring datasets through a variety of multivariate statistical techniques (McCune and Grace 2002).

The proposed revisit design change is simple and consistent with the revised bird community monitoring logistical plan. Here it is proposed that the logistical plan be modified so that plant community monitoring sites and invasive plant transects are measured for a single year followed by a three-year interval without sampling. This proposed change not only maintains the three-year window in which to initiate management activities originally afforded to park managers under the current revisit design, but it also extends that three-year window so that it is consistent with other terrestrial monitoring projects within a park. In other words, under the original revisit design there was a three-year window when plant community monitoring did not occur, but this window was not the same as that for bird community or invasive plant monitoring. Different or overlapping revisit schedules among terrestrial monitoring projects reduced the window a park manager had to initiate management activities in a year in which no HTLN monitoring occurred. Under the proposed design, each park will have a three-year window in which no bird or plant monitoring occurs. This increases the opportunity for a park manager to initiate management activities and for HTLN monitoring to measure a detectable response from monitoring sites among monitoring projects.

In addition, the proposed logistical plan will allow for additional monitoring to occur within a park as the need arises. Like the current logistical plan, the proposed design allows for the maximum number of sites to be monitored within a sample year. This change will not have a negative impact on the budget or increase trampling in communities (concerns put forth in support of the original logistical plan).

Initial HTLN effort was made to have spatial co-location of terrestrial monitoring sites within parks. The proposed logistical plan and revisit design will add temporal co-location of terrestrial monitoring sites at parks as well. This will result in consolidated and coordinated reporting across bird community and vegetation community monitoring efforts as well as invasive plant monitoring. Consolidation in preparing reports provides the most accurate and timely analysis to park managers. Furthermore, it aids in interpreting the impact of management activities or evaluating management objectives in areas that overlap among different monitoring projects (e.g., the goal of increasing woody species cover for breeding bird habitat while keeping woody species cover below a desired level for prairie plant community function).

The proposed changes to the logistical and revisit plan reflect initial protocol development in which it was stated that "efforts should be made to integrate vegetation community monitoring efforts with related monitoring components as data are collected" (Buck et al. 2000). Integrating monitoring components reflects the inherent integration of taxa and habitat within a functioning community.

Implementation Plan:

During the 2008 and 2009 field seasons the current and proposed logistical plan will overlap to complete currently scheduled monitoring at TAPR, AGFO and SCBL. During the 2008 field season the proposed schedule will begin with the Ozark-prairie tour, monitoring at WICR and GWCA. Transition to the proposed logistical plan and revisit design will be complete by 2010 (Table 1).

Table 1. Plant community monitoring proposed logistical plan that temporally coordinates bird community and invasive plant monitoring at the park scale. Monitoring will take place for one year followed by a three-year interval without sampling.

Tour	Region (Parks)	2008	2009	2010	2011	2012	2013	2014	2015	2016	2017	2018	2019	2020
1	Ozark-prairie (WICR–GWCA)	X				X				X				X
2	Prairie-savanna (HOME–PIPE–EFMO–HEHO)		X				X				X			
3	Tallgrass prairie (TAPR)		X		X^		X		X^			X	X^	
4	Deciduous forest (ARPO–LIBO–HOCU)				X				X				X	
5	Ozark-forest (WICR–PERI–HOSP)					X*				X				X*
6	Eastern forest (EFMO)	X	X	X X	X	X		X	X X	X	X		X	X

* = Understory only sampled.

^ = Patch burn-grazing monitoring

It is important to note that in 2006 a departure from the original revisit design occurred to assess the need for plant community monitoring at LIBO and HOCU. The proposed changes address plant community monitoring at these parks along with ARPO through extended analysis of bird habitat monitoring data. Initially habitat data collected during the breeding bird surveys at LIBO, HOCU and ARPO will be jointly analyzed by the wildlife ecologist and plant ecologist to assess the plant community of the parks based on habitat data (plant guild and vertical structure data) collected from bird monitoring sites. By building this sampling tour (Deciduous forest tour, table 1) into the proposed logistical plan, time has been allocated for plant community monitoring to increase at these three parks without disrupting the revisit design for other parks.

As indicated in Table 1, additional plant community monitoring will be conducted at TAPR, focusing entirely on the area under patch burn-grazing management. This departure from the current annual monitoring at TAPR is addressed below.

Logistical Plan Methodology:

The details of sampling within the proposed logistical plan remain unchanged from the current plan. The only specific change is the addition of sampling the prairie community at EFMO in the prairie-savanna tour, which includes HEHO, HOME and PIPE. Therefore operational efficiency is maintained in the proposed logistical plan.

In the event that it is inappropriate to monitor at a park during its scheduled year, every attempt will be made to sample during the next year. Prescribed burns or extreme weather events that occur immediately prior to the scheduled monitoring are two examples of events that would render monitoring inappropriate (resulting data would be considered outliers due to the unusual conditions under which they were collected). These types of events or scenarios are considered rare. Therefore the resulting additional sampling effort the following year should not impact the proposed logistical plan beyond a single sample year.

Revisit Plan Methodology:

The proposed changes to the revisit plan consist of a one-year-on, three-year-off schedule for plant community and invasive plant monitoring. This revisit design has two advantages over the current design: 1) bird and plant community monitoring projects are temporally coordinated in sampling, data analysis and reporting; and 2) environmental data sets are available to analyze in conjunction with community data to more accurately address variability in monitoring data without loss of information.

Proposed changes in the revisit design specific to TAPR: Currently TAPR is sampled annually. Initial reasoning to conduct annual plant community monitoring at TAPR centered on: 1) sampling-related trampling was minimal compared to trampling of the community by cattle and 2) intensive annual sampling formed part of ongoing research and design work (DeBacker et al. 2004).

Findings from trend analysis of plant community monitoring data from TAPR collected from 2002-2006 found a high level of homogeneity among sites and across sample years regardless of pasture or management (James and DeBacker 2007). Intensive annual sampling is most appropriate for understanding heterogeneity within a community over time (Buck et al. 2000). Initial long-term analysis of annual data from TAPR does not support continued annual sampling. However, a new management regime was undertaken in a portion of the upland prairies at TAPR beginning in 2006. Patch burn-grazing management was initiated in a portion of the park with the goal of increasing plant community structure. The current revisit design does not address patch burn-grazing. Here it is proposed that management-specific intensive sampling begin in those areas to address park-specific management goals. This trade-off between annual sampling and more focused intensive sampling provides greater benefit to the park managers than continued annual sampling.

In addition to management-specific intensive sampling of the patch burn-grazing area, we propose to increase the number of sites sampled across the park. In years in which sampling occurs across the upland prairies, additional sites will be added to increase spatial representation across the prairie. Some of these sites will also be part of the intensive management focused sampling that is scheduled to occur in the next successive year on the sampling calendar (Table 1). This additional sampling effort offsets the temporal reduction in sampling with increased spatial sampling, while addressing specific management actions directed at the plant community that are not currently being addressed.

Literature Cited:

Buck, C.E., G.D. Willson, L. Thomas, M. DeBacker. 2000. Background Information and Methods Testing for the Development of a Plant Community Protocol for Six Prairie Parks. National Park Service Document.

DeBacker, M.D., A.N. Sasseen, C. Becker, G.A. Rowell, L.P. Thomas, J.R. Boetsch, G.D. Willson. 2004. Vegetation Community Monitoring Protocol for the Heartland I&M Network and Prairie Cluster Prototype Monitoring Program. National Park Service Document.

James, K. and DeBacker, M. 2007. Plant Community Monitoring Trend Report, Tallgrass Prairie National Preserve. Natural Resource Technical Report NPS/HTLN/NRTR—2007/030. National Park Service, Fort Collins, Colorado.

Lesica, P. and B.M. Steele. 1996. A method for monitoring long-term population trends: an example using rare arctic-alpine plants. Ecological Applications 6 (3): 879 – 887.

McCune, B. and J. B. Grace. 2002. Analysis of Ecological Communities. MJM software Design.

Appendix B. Proposal to Change the Revisit Design for Prairie Communities in the Heartland Network.

Kevin James, Lloyd Morrison and Mike DeBacker

Executive Summary:

A goal of long-term monitoring in prairie communities is to track changes in density of species, along with species composition and distribution. Currently foliar cover estimates collected during two sample events within a single year are combined and used to measure change in species abundance. Recent work has resulted in an analytic method that fully utilizes nested frequency data. This method uses frequency data reported at the optimized scale for each species, which provides a more accurate surrogate for inferring and monitoring change in species density through time. Employing this method no longer requires warm season foliar cover estimates, rather only frequency measures that can be obtained earlier in the growing season. The proposed change to the prairie community revisit design will result in better estimates of species density while reducing personnel time and costs. Here it is proposed to reduce the sampling of prairie communities to include only the cool season sample event for each sample year. This change would eliminate the second sample event of the revisit design while keeping the timing of the cool season event unchanged.

Introduction:

Conducting long-term monitoring of prairie plant communities requires an understanding of both cool season and warm season components that make up the total species richness within a growing season. Plant species that flower early in the growing season (usually before July) are referred to as cool season plants, while those that flower later in the season (July and after) are labeled as warm season plants. Here 'cool' and 'warm' are related to the late spring/early summer and later summer temperatures displayed in the prairies during different times of the year. The designation of cool and warm season plants has been extended to label the two sample events within a sample year for HTLN monitoring in prairie communities. Typically, due to time and budget restrictions, prairies are sampled only once during a growing season and thus a concession is made as to which information is important and contributes to the overall goals and objectives of the project. Fortunately, the prairie communities in the HTLN have been sampled during both the cool and warm seasons for a number of years.

The rationale for sampling the prairie communities a second time (during the warm season) was: 1) to provide the most accurate estimation of foliar cover for warm season grasses and 2) to sample late summer/early fall forb species (DeBacker et al. 2004). Warm season grasses are those species that define a prairie (big and little bluestem, Indian grass, panic grass, gamma grasses). Originally, cover estimates of abundance were to be used to infer density of individual species and to provide an overview of the core species in the prairie.

Recent simulation work involving HTLN monitoring data indicates that a narrow range of frequency data is a better surrogate than foliar cover estimates for inferring changes in density of prairie species (Heywood and DeBacker 2007). Subsequent HTLN plant community monitoring data analysis methods were developed to fully utilize all of the frequency information that is collected in the nested sampling design. The original goal of using warm season abundance data to infer change in species density is now addressed with species nested frequency data, which has different requirements than cover estimates for ensured data collection accuracy and consistency.

Here it is proposed that the logistical plan for sampling prairie communities within a sample year be reduced to only the single late spring / early summer sample event. The proposed change is based on HTLN monitoring data collected over the past 10 years from three prairie parks and will not diminish the quality of community data previously collected under the current logistical plan. Furthermore, this proposal will have a dramatic positive impact on the plant community monitoring budget by concentrating prairie sampling into a single sample event. This consolidation will in turn simplify data management and increase the integrity of all statistical analyses and reporting.

Each sample event, regardless of timing within the sample year, requires the same amount of personnel and time. Therefore the sampling effort (time and cost) is doubled for two sampling events. Data from TAPR core prairie sites, HOME restored prairie, PIPE native prairie and PIPE restored prairie (Figs. 1 – 4, respectively) illustrate the paucity of unique species sampled during the warm season (second trip during the year) as compared to those species unique to the cool season sampling and those species common to both sample events.

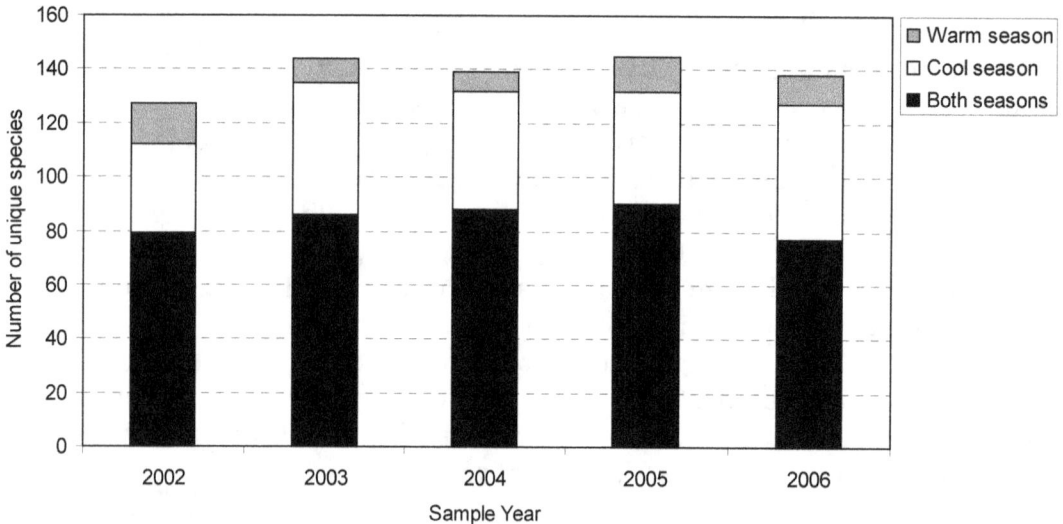

Figure 1. Composite count of unique species sampled at TAPR either in both seasons, only the cool season and only the warm season for all core sites (n = 23) for 2002 – 2006.

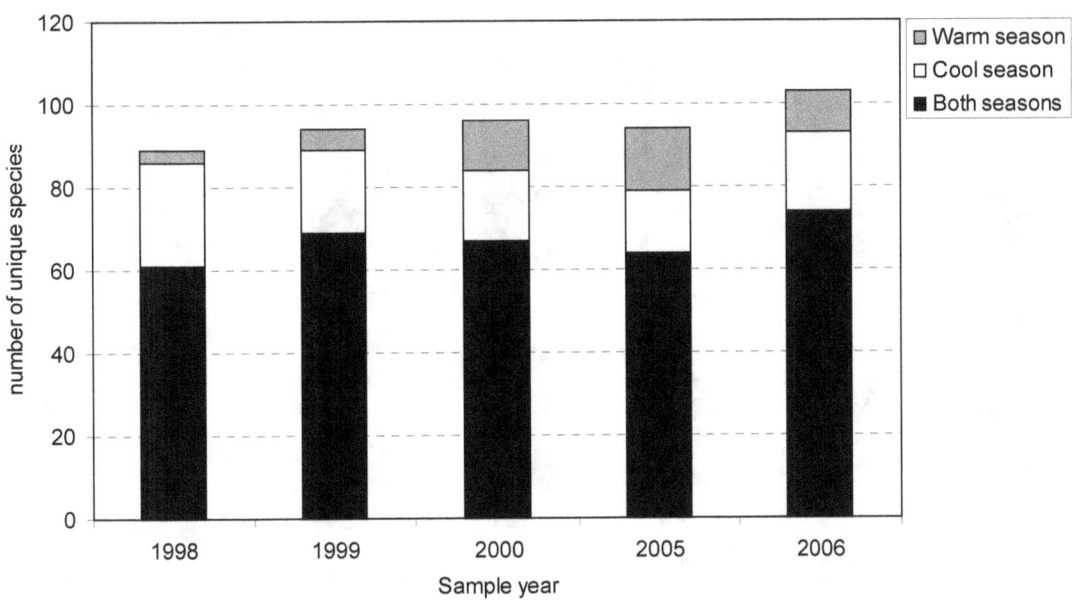

Figure 2. Composite count of unique species sampled in the restored prairie at HOME either in both seasons, only the cool season and only the warm season for all core sites (n = 5) for 1998 – 2006.

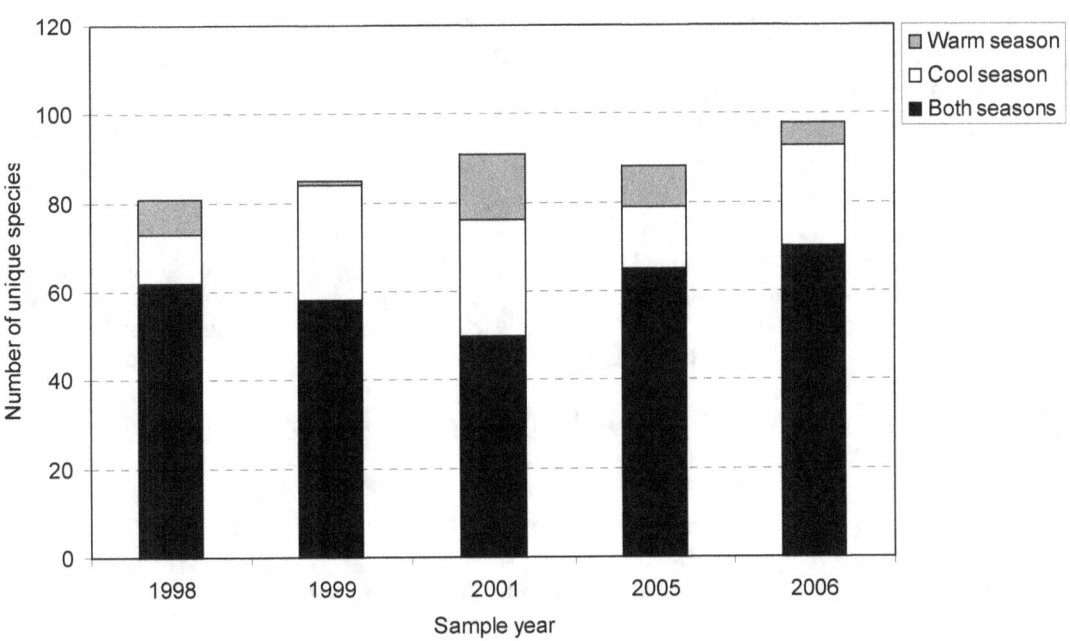

Figure 3. Composite count of unique species sampled in the native prairie at PIPE either in both seasons, only the cool season and only the warm season for all core sites (n = 4) for 1998 – 2006.

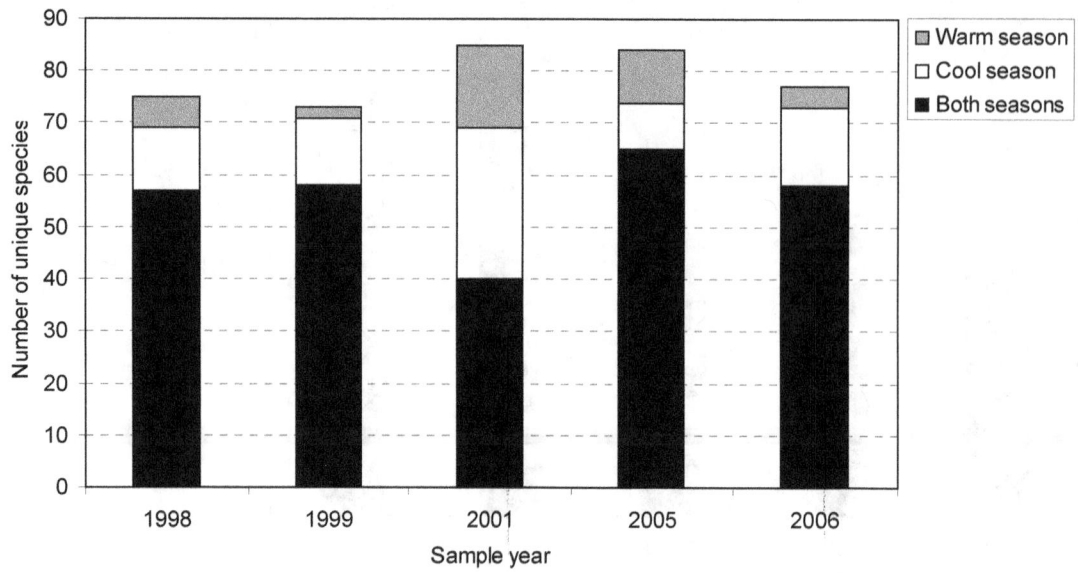

Figure 4. Composite count of unique species sampled in the restored prairie at PIPE either in both seasons, only the cool season and only the warm season for all core sites (n = 3) for 1998 – 2006.

The figures above provide a clear example of the amount of species composition overlap between the two sample seasons within a year (solid black bars on Figs. 1 - 4). A doubling of monitoring effort within a field season to conduct both cool season and warm season sampling does not produce proportional information for the effort and cost (Table 1). The mean annual gain in species richness across cool and warm season sample events for all three parks never exceeds 10%. Moreover, those additional species do not contribute to understanding the integrity and function of the prairie community beyond increasing species richness and subsequent evenness calculations.

Table 1. Total species richness (mean count ± 1 standard deviation), richness of species sampled in the warm season only (mean count ± 1 standard deviation) and the resulting unique warm season species percent of the total richness (mean percent ± 1 standard deviation) across all sample years for each park and prairie community within park. Site refers to the number of monitoring sites within the park and community.

Park: prairie community	Site (n)	Total species	Warm season species*	Percent of total
TAPR	23	138.6 (7.2)	11 (3.2)	8.0 (2.6)
HOME	5	95.2 (5.1)	9 (5.0)	9.4 (5.1)
PIPE: Native	4	88.6 (6.4)	7.6 (5.2)	8.6 (5.8)
PIPE: Restored	3	78.8 (5.4)	7.6 (5.5)	9.3 (6.3)

* = only species not able to be accurately and consistently identified in the cool season

Species diversity metrics, such as Evenness, Shannon diversity index and Simpson's diversity index, are affected by changes in total species richness. Therefore the major impact of the proposed change would be expressed in the calculated diversity metrics. This was a concern of the authors when considering such a change to the revisit design. Comparing the three diversity metrics indicated little effect of the reduced species richness when analyzing only the cool season sample event as compared to both sample events (Table 2). This indicates that most species detected only during the second sample event are not abundant species and thus have little impact on overall species diversity in the community.

Table 2. Comparison of three measures of diversity between cool season only revisit design (cool) and two sample event revisit design (both) for each community within park. Mean (standard deviation) for sample years (n = 4) is presented for each diversity metric.

Park Prairie		Evenness		Shannon diversity index		Simpson's diversity index	
		cool	both	cool	both	cool	both
PIPE Native		0.857	0.858	3.74	3.89	0.966	0.972
		(0.014)	(.011)	(0.05)	(0.08)	(0.002)	(0.002)
PIPE Restore	d	0.865	0.855	3.71	3.81	0.964	0.967
		(0.017)	(0.004)	(0.07)	(0.05)	(0.004)	(0.001)
HOME Restore	d	0.839	0.829	3.71	3.79	0.961	0.964
		(0.009)	(0.008)	(0.04)	(0.05)	(0.001)	(0.004)

It is because of new analytical methods that fully utilize the HTLN sampling design that we are able to make the proposed change that in fact increases the value and information content of the plant community monitoring data. Without these new methods, simply dropping one of the seasonal sampling events would not be appropriate, for that would not address the original goal of monitoring the inferred change in prairie species density through time. Recently developed data summary methods for analyzing nested frequency data better address change in abundance of warm season grasses than foliar cover estimates collected during a second sample event. As the park managers are informed by HTLN monitoring results, so is HTLN staff as reflected in a better understanding of how best to monitor the change in communities over time.

Within Season Revisit Design Methodology:

To obtain the most accurate foliar cover estimate, it is best to sample during the time in the growing season when the species is at its apex of growth for the year. This comes earlier in the season for some species than others, so cool season and warm season sampling resulted in more accurate and representative foliar cover estimates across the growing season than a single sampling event. Even though sampling twice in a growing season provided good foliar cover estimates, it has resulted in numerous problems for data management and data analysis, as described below. Accurate and consistent foliar cover estimates rely on both positive identification of the species and proper estimates of foliar cover at the 10 m^2 plot frame. Nested frequency data only requires positive identification of the species for all nested plot frames. Furthermore, the species must be at a growth stage where informative taxonomic characters are visible to ensure positive identification, which for most species does not require the species to be fully mature or at maximum growth. The seasonal requirements (cool vs. warm) are not critical to collect accurate and consistent frequency data across prairie communities in HTLN parks within a growing season (Table 2).

Table 2. Proposed sample season for HTLN parks grouped into sample tours.

Region	National Parks	Sample Season
Ozark prairie tour	WICR–GWCA	6/1 – 6/30
Prairie-savanna tour	EFMO–HEHO–HOME–PIPE	6/1 – 6/30
Tallgrass prairie tour	TAPR	5/1 – 5/31
Ozark-forest tour	WICR–PERI–HOSP	7/1 – 7/31
Eastern forest tour	EFMO	7/1 – 7/31

It is problematic at best and misleading at worst to collect data from two different points in time and combine the individual datasets for analysis as a single sample event. Managing such a database requires advanced knowledge of database design and constant vigilance to ensure consistent datasets are generated for further analysis and reporting. So far HTLN has avoided some of these pitfalls with minor impact on the data. As more data are collected through time, however, the ability to detect real community change will be confounded by the necessity to combine two sample events into a single dataset. One problematic scenario involves having a combined dataset that draws frequency data from one sample event and the maximum cover estimate for the same species from the other sample event. Although the impact on the outcome is minor, this subtle difference in reporting species frequency and abundance for a given year has the ability to either mask real change or indicate change that does not exist when looking at differences through time.

Optimized Frequency Methodology:

The proper metrics to use when addressing questions involving changes in density within a community are apparent only after the underlying species distributional patterns in prairie communities are known. The core-satellite species hypothesis can be applied to the community structure of prairie ecosystems (Hanski 1982, Collins and Glenn 1990). The spatial structure of species within the community reflects regionally common and locally abundant species (core species) that are widely distributed in the community and those species (satellite species) that are infrequent and patchily distributed throughout the community. Core species are more frequently encountered in the sampling design than satellite species as a result of their distributional patterns. Prairie spatial structure (changes in population density) can be measured at the community level by tracking the abundance and distribution of core and satellite species through time. Core and satellite species, due to different patterns of abundance and distribution, respond differently to stochastic variability and therefore when analyzed separately can aid in understanding changes in community structure and local density.

Long-term monitoring of plant communities has a specific goal of estimating the rate of temporal change as related to management efforts (DeBacker et al. 2004). Community changes are measured through community composition and species distribution. Addressing species distribution and the underlying changes in population structure are inferred from frequency data. Frequency data collected in a nested sampling design and reported as the optimized frequency for each species result in an estimate of population density that is both easy to interpret and appropriate for evaluating management actions.

Literature Cited:

Collins, S.L. and S.M. Glenn. 1990. A hierarchical analysis of species' abundance patterns in grassland vegetation. The American Naturalist 135: 633-648.

DeBacker, M.D., A.N. Sasseen, C. Becker, G.A. Rowell, L.P. Thomas, J.R. Boetsch, G.D. Willson. 2004. Vegetation Community Monitoring Protocol for the Heartland I&M Network and Prairie Cluster Prototype Monitoring Program. National Park Service Document.

Hanski, I. 1982. Dynam ics of regional distributi on: the core and satellite species hypothesis. Oikos 38: 210-221.

Heywood, J.S. and M.D. DeBacker. 2007. Optim   al Sam pling Designs for Monitoring P   lant Frequency. Rangeland Ecology and Management 60(4).

Appendix C. Park Reference Frames with Vegetation Site Locations.

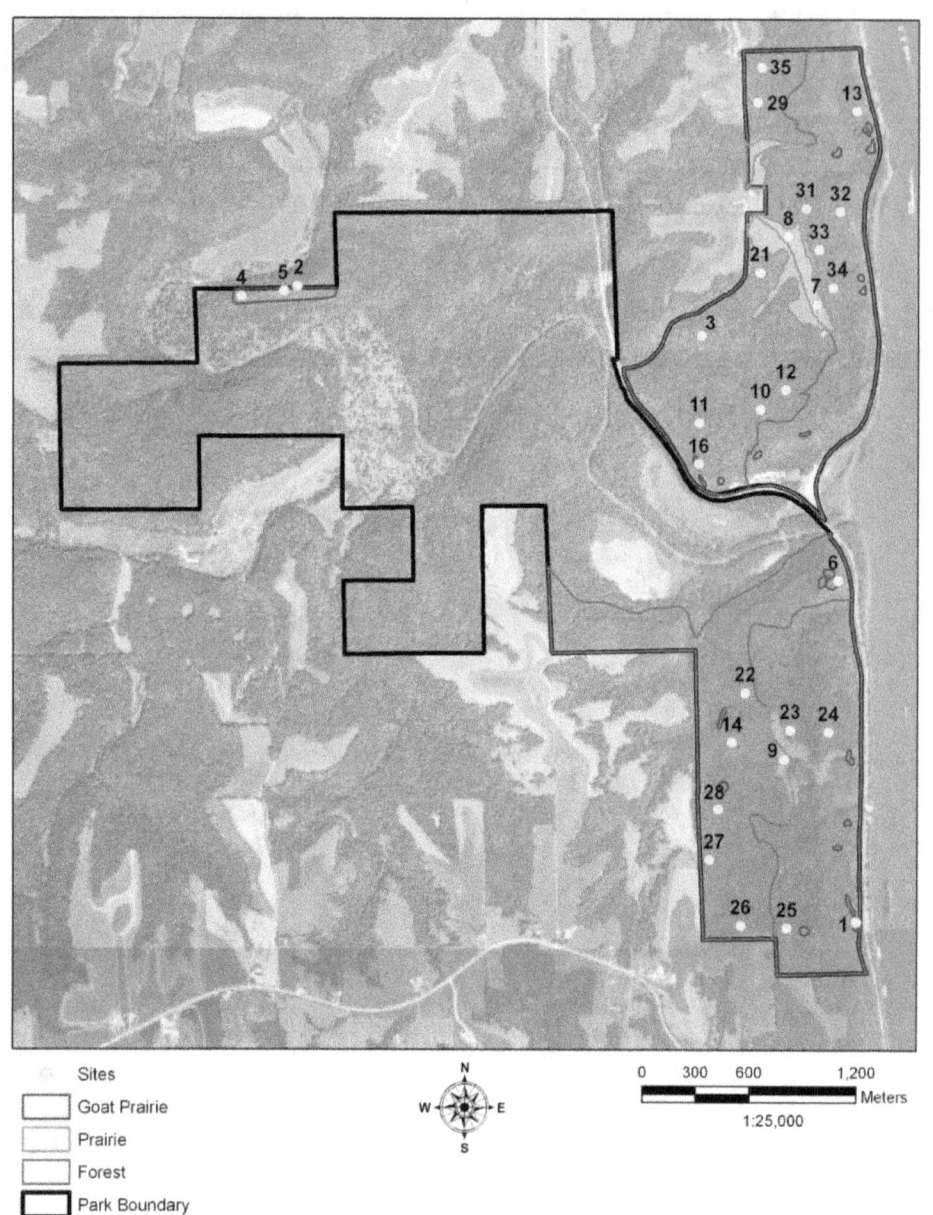

Figure C.1. Heartland Network reference frame and vegetation monitoring sites at Effigy Mounds National Monument, Iowa.

Sites

Restoration

Park Boundary

N
W · E
S

0   75   150   300
                        Meters
         1:6,000

Figure C.2. Heartland Network reference frame and vegetation monitoring sites at George Washington Carver National Monument, Missouri.

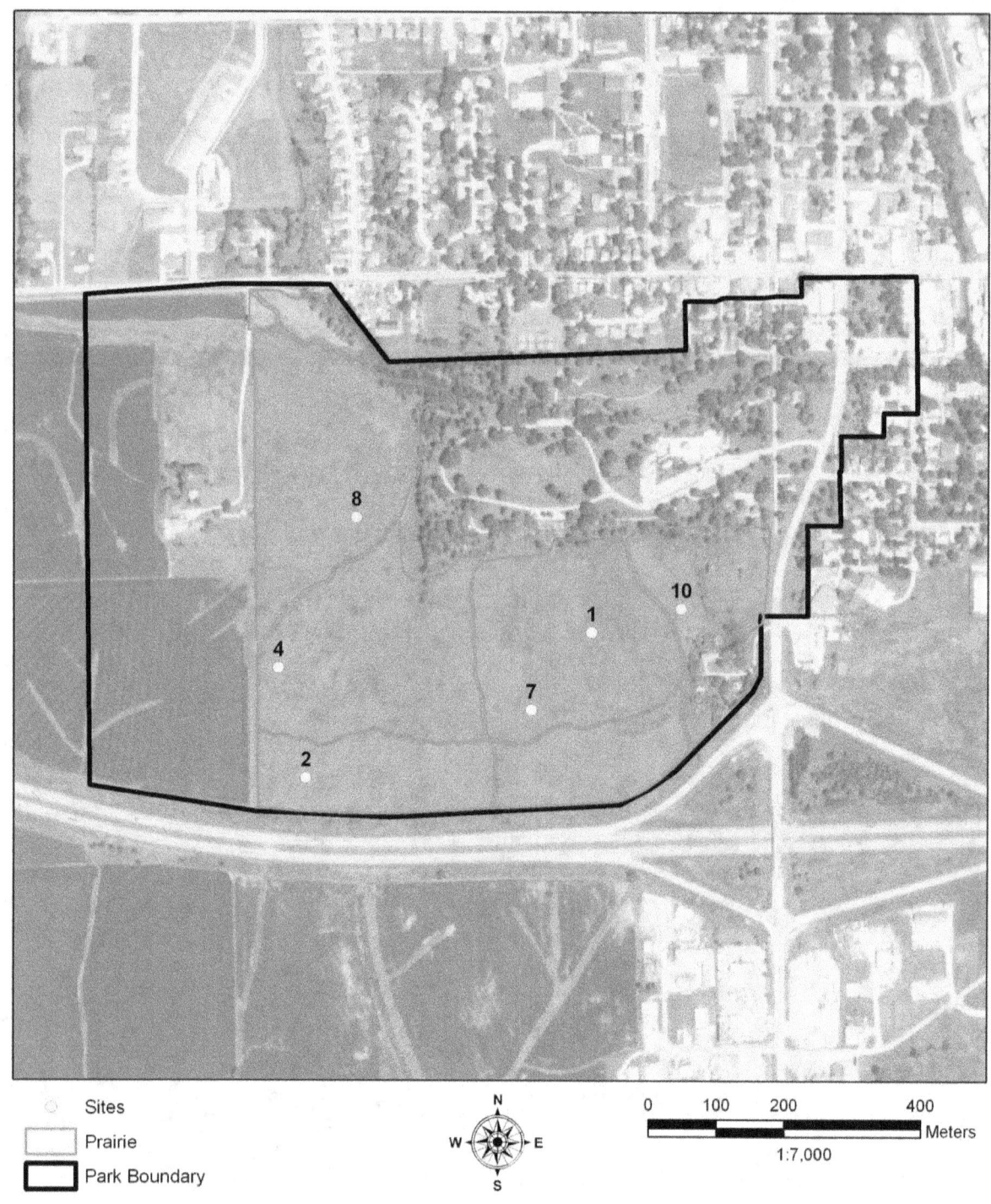

Figure C.3. Heartland Network reference frame and vegetation monitoring sites at Herbert Hoover National Historic Site, Iowa.

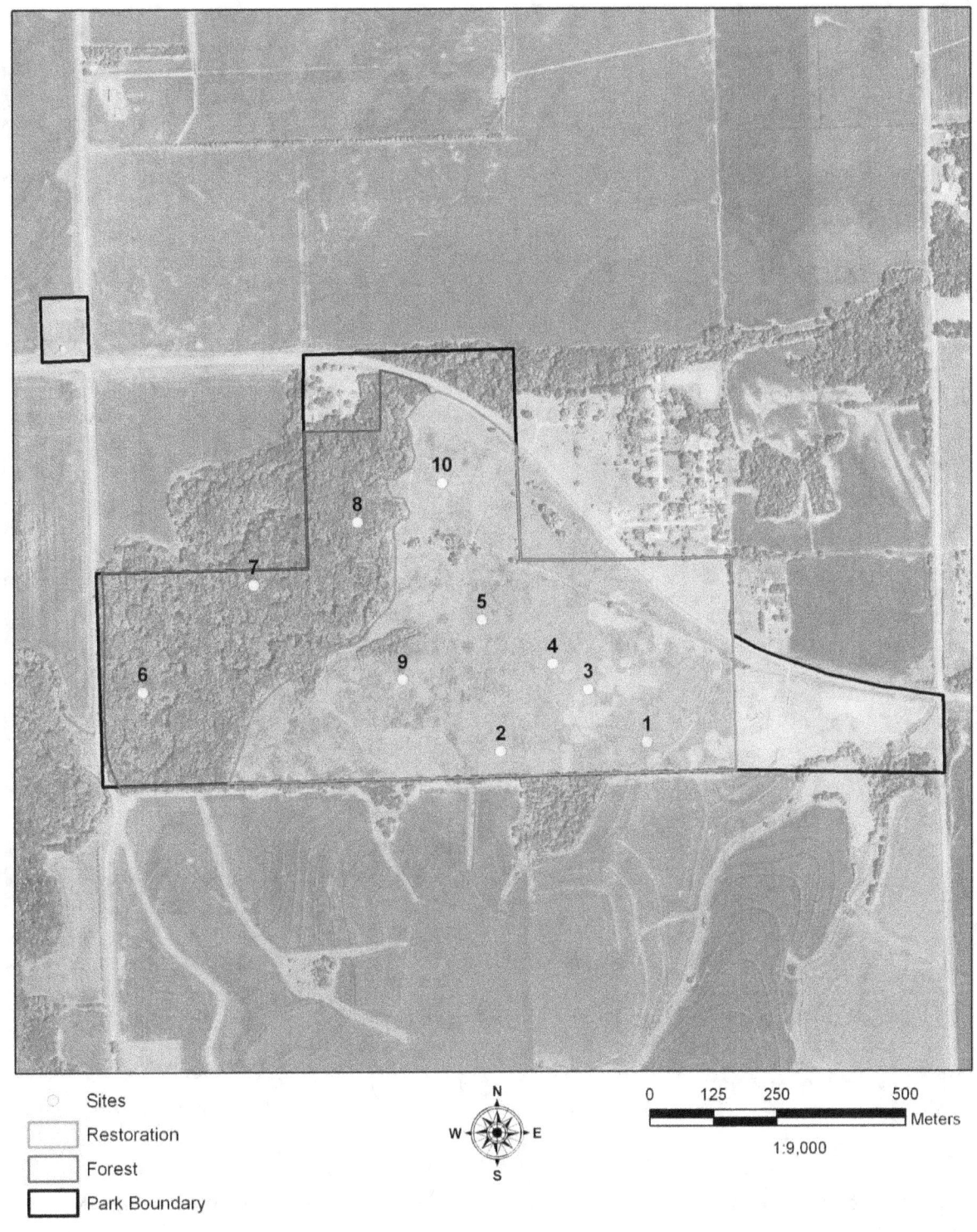

Figure C.4. Heartland Network reference frame and vegetation monitoring sites at Homestead National Monument of America, Nebraska.

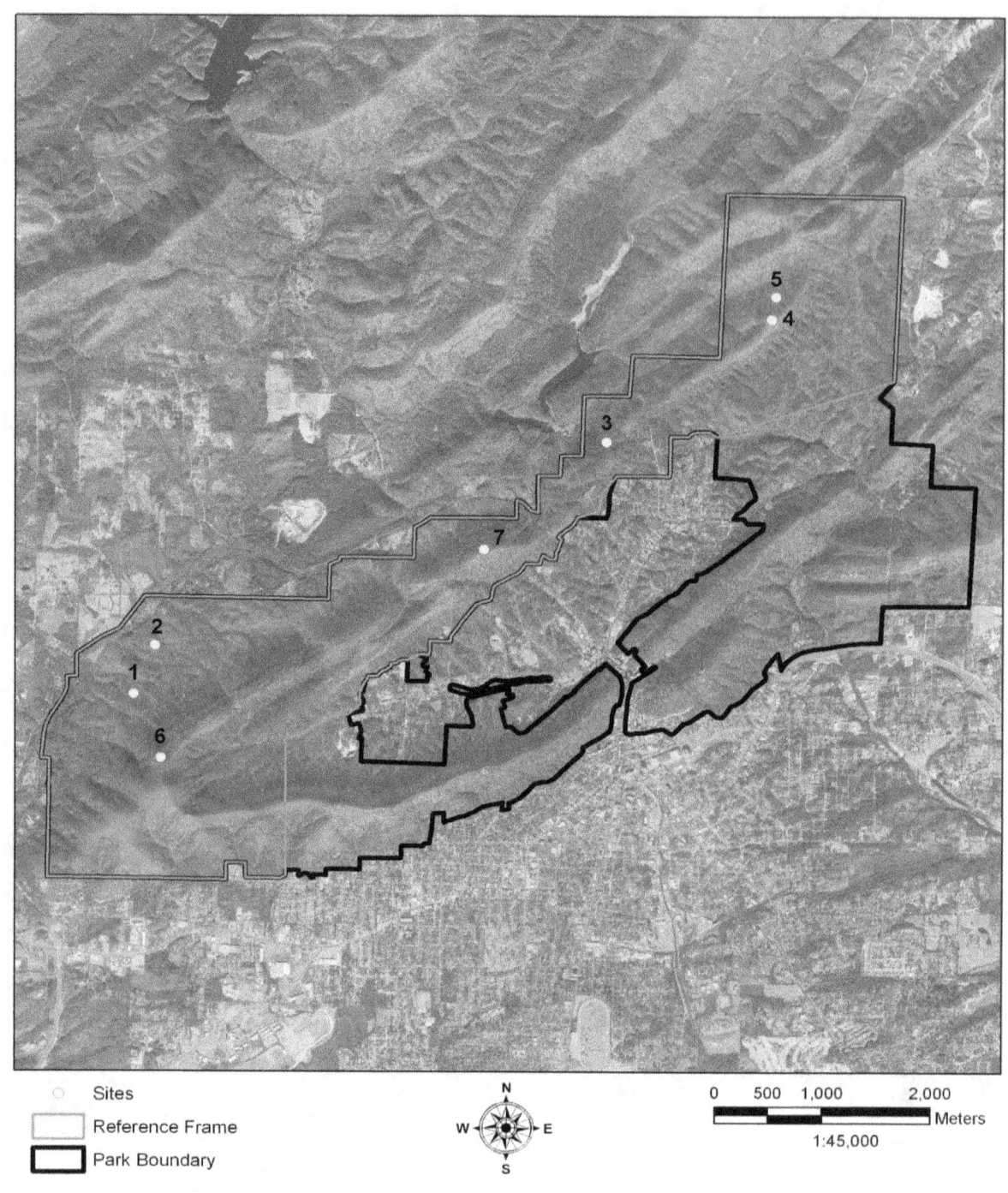

Figure C.5. Heartland Network reference frame and vegetation monitoring sites at Hot Springs National Park, Arkansas.

100

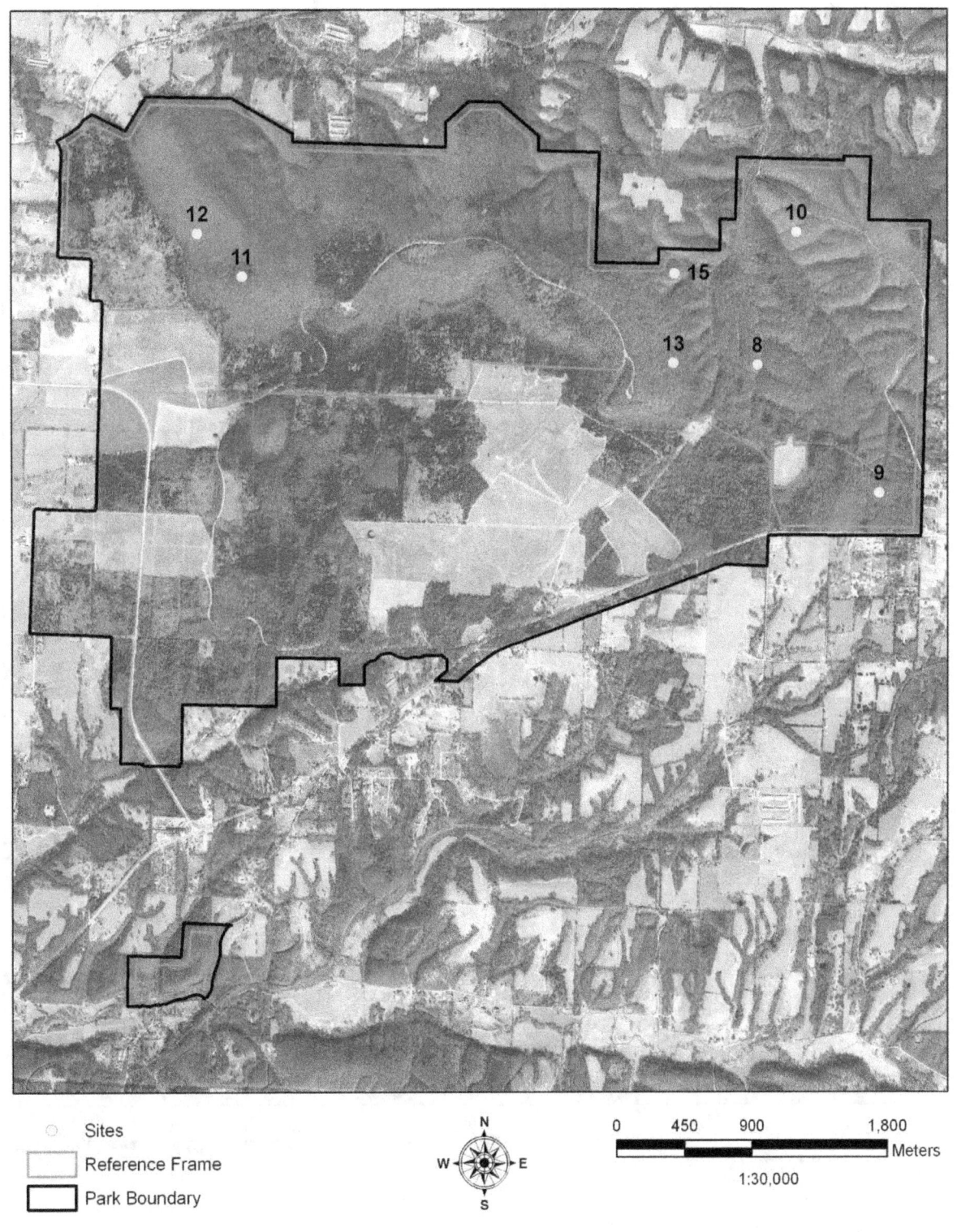

Figure C.6. Heartland Network reference frame and vegetation monitoring sites at Pea Ridge National Military Park, Arkansas.

Figure C.7. Heartland Network reference frame and vegetation monitoring sites at Pipestone National Monument, Minnesota.

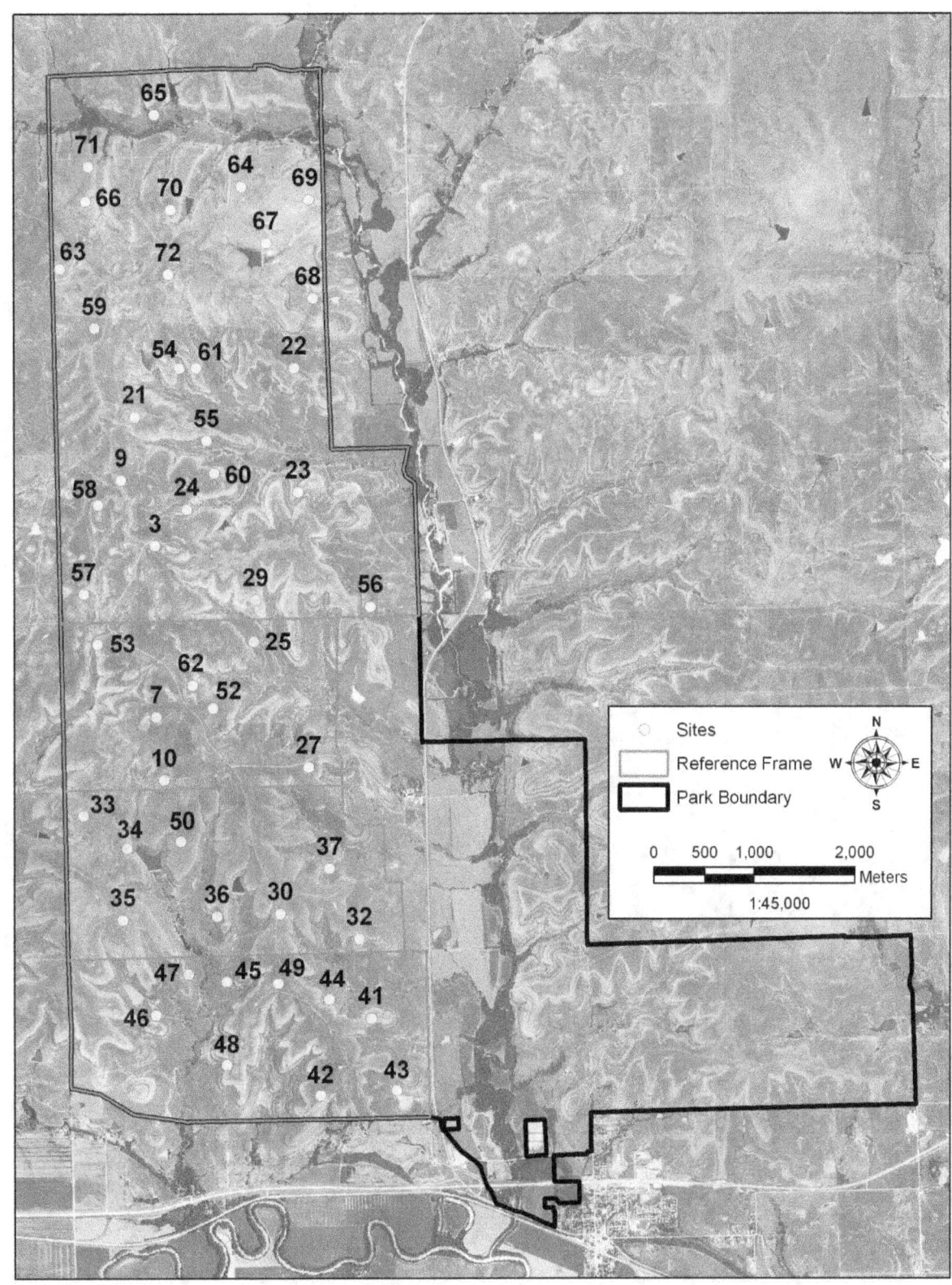

Figure C.8. Heartland Network reference frame and vegetation monitoring sites at Tallgrass Prairie National Preserve, Kansas.

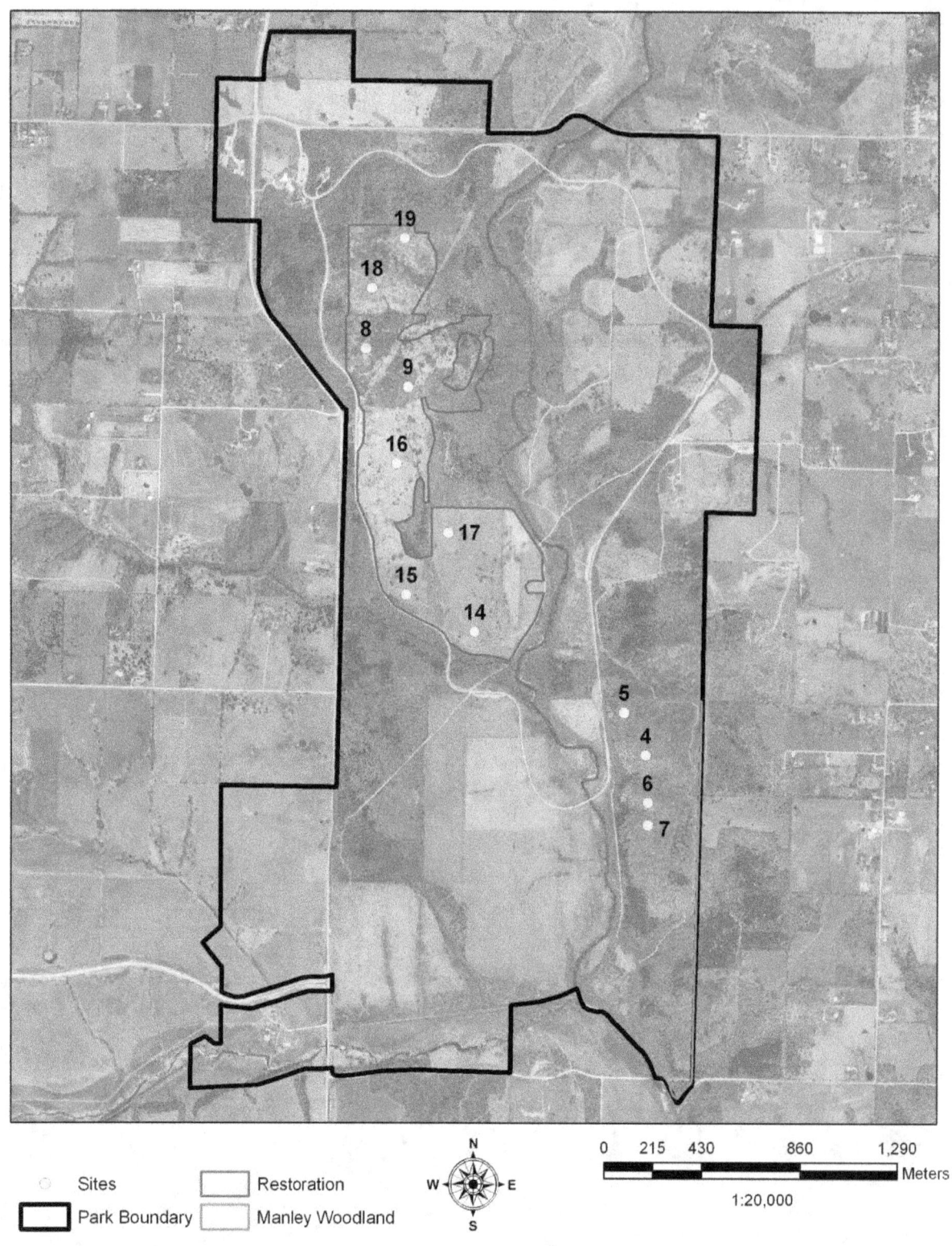

Figure C.9. Heartland Network reference frame and vegetation monitoring sites at Wilson's Creek National Battlefield, Missouri.

NPS 920/100249, August 2009